Rax King is the James Beard Award–nominated
author of *Tacky* and cohost of the podcast *Low
Culture Boil*. Her writing can be found in *Glamour*, *Bon Appétit*, *Food & Wine,* and elsewhere. She
lives in Brooklyn with her husband and toothless
Pekingese.

Sloppy

Or: Doing It All Wrong

Rax King

Vintage Books

A Division of Penguin Random House LLC

New York

A VINTAGE BOOKS ORIGINAL 2025

Copyright © 2025 by Rax King

Published by Vintage Books, 1745 Broadway, New York, NY 10019.

Vintage and colophon are registered trademarks of
Penguin Random House LLC.

Some names and identifying details have been changed to protect the
privacy of individuals.

Library of Congress Cataloging-in-Publication Data
Names: King, Rax, author.
Title: Sloppy : or: doing it all wrong / Rax King.
Description: First edition. | New York : Vintage Books, 2025.
Identifiers: LCCN 2024030374 (print) | LCCN 2024030375 (ebook) |
    ISBN 978-0-593-68845-8 (paperback) | ISBN 978-0-593-68846-5 (ebook)
Subjects: LCSH: King, Rax. | Women authors, American—Biography. |
    Alcoholics—United States—Biography.
Classification: LCC PS3611.I58425 Z46 2025 (print) |
    LCC PS3611.I58425 (ebook) | DDC 814/.6 B—dc23/eng/2025047
LC record available at https://lccn.loc.gov/2024030374
LC record available at https://lccn.loc.gov/2024030375

Vintage Books Trade Paperback ISBN: 978-0-593-68845-8
eBook ISBN: 978-0-593-68846-5

Book design by Steven Walker

penguinrandomhouse.com | vintagebooks.com

Printed in the United States of America
1st Printing

The authorized representative in the EU for product safety and compliance
is Penguin Random House Ireland, Morrison Chambers, 32 Nassau Street,
Dublin D02 YH68, Ireland, https://eu-contact.penguin.ie.

For my mother, who taught me how to be sober even when I plugged my ears and sang "nah-nah-nah-nah" in the hopes that I wouldn't hear her

Hank, why do you drink?
Hank, why do you roll smoke?
Why must you live out the songs that you wrote?
— Hank Williams Jr., "Family Tradition"

. . . TO GET DRUNK!
. . . TO GET HIGH!
. . . TO GET LAID!
— traditional audience response to
Hank Williams Jr.'s "Family Tradition"

Contents

Sloppy   3

Proud Alcoholic Stock   17

Shoplifting from Brandy Melville   33

Pants on Fire   43

The Temple of Feminine Perfection   59

Anger Management   79

Ten Items   92

Your Pet Is Dying: An Online Life   102

Ms. Girl Power   120

Cough-Cough   135

Front of House   146

Bad Friend   166

Up from Sloth   184

Some Notes Towards a Theory of an Old Dad   196

Hey Big Spender   207

Commitment Issues   224

Domesticating the Wolf of Wall Street   246

Acknowledgments   259

Sloppy

Sloppy

Selected reasons I have skipped class, from elementary school through senior year of college:

- "Best of Maury" marathon airing that afternoon
- Free pancake day at IHOP
- Sad over a breakup
- Too happy about a breakup to waste my good mood on class
- Seat of pants ripped when I pulled them on, gave up on the day
- Hungover
- Still drunk
- Ex-husband (generally)
- Spaghetti took longer than expected to cook
- Wanted to watch my father argue a case, knew he would cover for me if I blew enough smoke up his ass
- *L'ennui*
- Spider on alarm clock
- Roommate used the last coffee filter
- Not sure what this means but I found a diary entry that says I skipped class because of "Gerald" so it must have happened

It was 2008, and I was surprised that it had taken until junior year for my class-cutting to get me in trouble. This may have been a function of the hippie-dippie high school I attended, where we were graded according to an innovative rubric of mirror affirmations and kisses on the forehead, but still—I'd been skipping at least a day a week for two years. All my classes had about ten kids in them. Had it taken the school this long to notice, or had they assumed until now that I'd been out there expressing myself and was therefore not to be bothered?

Dianne from the dean's office searched my face for signs of contrition. (Every employee at that school, from the dean's office to the custodial crew to the faculty members, was known to us by their first name.) The school had dispatched Dianne to discipline me, and she clearly did not want to. Not because she was incapable of being a hard-ass, mind you. Loosey-goosey as the place was, she was a *high school administrator*—"hard-ass" was her mother tongue. No; I realized as Dianne sat before me looking defeated in her full-body Chico's that she had thought better of me. Maybe that was why it had taken the school so long to discipline me. Based on my meek personality, they believed I was a good student. It had taken two full years of incontrovertible evidence to convince them otherwise.

"I'm sorry," I mumbled for what must have been the fifth time that meeting. I'm sure I looked it, too. I liked Dianne. She wasn't warm and fuzzy, which I respected. She didn't act like a teenager the way some of our teachers did, the ones who'd begun teaching here because business school hadn't worked out or they couldn't get hired at Lockheed. Unlike them, she was patently *not* one of us, and we benefited from it. Her prim sturdiness felt like it belonged to a different time and place—*Grease*'s Rydell High, say.

Dianne nodded and then slumped down in her chair. I was draining her. "Don't let it happen again. The only reason this meeting isn't ending in a suspension is that we all know you're better than this."

The problem was, and would forever be, that I *wasn't* better than this. No, I wasn't a mouthy punk who would make a scene in class and then catch both a suspension and a Ritalin prescription. Dianne's job may not have been easy in those cases, but it was clear-cut. Not so with quiet fuckups like me, and I'd been exploiting that happy loophole for two years. After all, I never bullied anyone or cussed in class. I'd never made less than an A in English, and even as I turned in consistently sloppy work in every other class, I was at least quiet enough to ignore. Who were they going to punish? Me, or the guy who used a lit Bunsen burner to set his kid sister's Barbie on fire?

As far as I know, nobody from the school ever did call my parents. Or else maybe they only called my dad, who would have absorbed the information intending to punish me and then forgotten about it as soon as he hung up the phone, because he was a sloppy fuckup, too.

Bosses, teachers, and administrators all believe in my quality as an underling. They ignore any evidence to its contrary for as long as they can, and then they *might* slap my wrist. Why? Because I'm soft-spoken, punctual, and forthcoming with the "sirs" and "ma'ams"—those are the only reasons I can think of, because in no other way am I a good employee or student. I'm not just a bad underling, either—I'm a slob of a friend, girlfriend, and wife. Where other brains are organized systems of folds, mine is a bowl of lukewarm soup. The truth is I always wanted to be sharp and orderly so badly. I just didn't know where to begin.

It hadn't always been this way. Not to brag or anything, but I *breezed* through addition and subtraction back in elementary school. Until fourth grade or so, I was like the stupidly named Will Hunting in the unconscionably stupidly named *Good Will Hunting:* school, unlike sports or friends, just made sense to me. I couldn't have explained it and never thought to ask questions about it.

Certainly there were kids who struggled, who wore their sloppiness on the surface. Remember the ADHD Lad? If you attended elementary school between 1990 and 2010 you would have seen him: a beloved class-clown type, good-natured, whip-smart, male, druglessly tweaking at his desk every day because he was *not* Will Hunting, school did *not* make sense to him. He wasn't necessarily tall, but his vivaciousness added inches to his height and decibels to his voice. I mentioned him in his advanced, mutated form above, the mouthy punk getting suspended for the Bunsen burner incident. That's what happened to the ADHD Lad if his symptoms weren't caught early—or, frankly, if he wasn't white.

In third grade, the ADHD Lad par excellence was one Elliott Meisner. His favorite pastime was drawing comics in which he appeared as the protagonist, Smelliott. When he was called upon to read a few sentences aloud in class, he always did so in a Groucho Marx voice or with a British accent—anything, anything to liven up those miserable reading primers.

"Wonderful imagination, Elliott," said the teacher every time, while we tittered. "But where in the text are you getting the idea that the person speaking has an accent?"

In the text?! What a stupid question. That idea *wasn't* in the text, which was a cold dead thing, prim black letters oozing drear all over every page. No, the idea came straight from Elliott's noodle, and he had been gracious enough to share it with us. If anything, we should be thanking him.

I desperately *wanted* to pay attention to whatever my teachers were saying about, I don't know, the Spanish-American War probably. (Anytime you can't remember what your teachers were blathering on about, it was the Spanish-American War. Doesn't it just sound like the kind of lesson you zoned out for?) The ADHD Lad must have desperately wanted to pay attention, too. He acted out and I caved in. Every period of every class for years, the same thing: I listened dutifully for thirty seconds at a time and then something else grabbed my focus, the sound of the rain on the roof, say, or the compulsion to doodle yet another long-lashed eye on my page. All dreamy girls doodle The Eye, this faceless orb with long horsey lashes and a badly shaded iris. If I tried to listen doodlelessly, I had to squirm; if I couldn't squirm, I had to grind my teeth; and during the two years I had a retainer and couldn't grind, my grades were at their absolute worst.

I felt awful about all this, understand. There was nothing adversarial in my feelings towards these teachers who took my

Eye away or asked my parents to sign my failed quizzes. I adored teachers—any teacher, it didn't matter. They were all my mommies and I didn't want to disappoint them. They adored me, too, even the ones giving me D-minuses. They didn't want to keep scrawling *SLOPPY!* on my tests in red pen any more than I wanted to keep reading it. I had a real old-lady-at-the-seder energy about me, and how do you give a failing grade to a grandma?

Teachers told me, in essence, to nut up and just get the damn work done. *Study,* they said. *Slow down, stop making sloppy mistakes.* Which was all well and good, only: How?

As far as I understood it, "studying" was pure mysticism. I was meant to stare at my schoolbook for an hour and . . . absorb its contents, somehow? Through osmosis, through sorcery? I suppose the idea was to *read* the book, which I did, and did joyfully, anytime the prose was hot and the story lively. But that kind of reading bore no resemblance to what I sat at my kitchen table and did with doorstops like *BIOLOGY: Vol. 1* or *Precalculus Mathematics for Calculus Second Edition Learn Calculus.* Even their titles were all business. Was it too much to ask that the dorks who authored these megillahs at least *try* to spiff up the writing a little?

I only applied to a single college, which was known for two things: its academic Program, a curriculum of Great Books from the Western canon (which I liked); and its 80 percent acceptance rate (which I liked even more). Best of all, the school had no exams, meaning no humiliating documents on which my educators could scrawl *SLOPPY!* The place ran half on intellectual rigor and half on gimmicks, e.g. its annual lawn croquet game against the midshipmen of the Naval Academy and its self-important perma-capitalization of the word "Program." It might have been a cult. The school's high acceptance rate was a dare: *Sure, you can get in, but how long can you last?*

I responded to this dare by whipping around and around myself, a neurotic tornado gathering external problems I could solve instead of focusing on school. Drug addiction, a sick father, a cruel husband—these troubles were real, and I felt guilty for also getting a lot of use out of them. For example, would I have devoted my weekends to my ailing father so consistently if doing so didn't mean I could skip my Friday afternoon class to catch the last bus to D.C.?

"Skip your class?" my father said on the phone. "No, no, don't worry, then. I have a couple friends coming by this weekend anyway."

"Please! Those guys can't even cook a turkey sandwich. Let me come over! I'll bring chili."

There was a brief silence on the other end while my father wrestled between his love for good grades and his love for chili. "Well, maybe you get a ride from Kelly? Don't go missing any classes on my account."

Kelly was a school friend who had a car. I deeply regretted ever telling my father about her. "Kelly says she can't drive me tonight," I lied. "She has a . . . boat ride. With her uncle. From Anatevka."

Not my finest work, and there was a time when my father—

a professional-grade liar himself—would have cross-examined me until I crumbled, weeping and apologizing. Nobody had a better nose for my bullshit. But on this day he was too sick or too tired to notice. "Don't forget the chili," he said, ceding the game.

When I got to his house later, two quarts of his favorite chili in my overnight bag, he looked crabby.

"Did Kelly really have plans tonight?" he asked. "Because I'm thinking about what you said on the phone for three hours now, and I'm pretty sure that was just the end of *Fiddler on the Roof.*"

I was lying because I wanted to see him more than I wanted to haltingly read Greek strophes out loud, but also because I was drowning in schoolwork I didn't know how to do, didn't even know how to ask for help with. And the further my schoolwork got away from me, the worse my other problems got. I learned quickly that nothing takes the edge off of one's underwhelming academic performance like a bourbon-and-cocaine cocktail, and if said cocktail actually made the academic performance even worse in the medium-to-long run, that was nobody's business but my own. As long as I could convince my parents I was holding things together, I would, in fact, *be* holding things together—a fantasy that comforted me well enough until my terrible grades forced me to drop out and move back in with my mother.

She was, at that time, twenty years sober, and she could smell the addiction on me. Literally, sometimes, in the form of well whiskey or vomit. Her competence and resourcefulness were endless, and I should have simply confessed to her, since I knew as well as she did that I had a problem. Instead, the whole time we lived together, her competence had nowhere to go and festered into paranoia. A symptomatic exchange:

"You're on something. What are you on?"

"What? No, I'm not."

[angrily] "I'm not angry! I'm not! I just need to know what you're on. Your pupils are huge. Look at how you're sweating!"

"Well, yeah, it's July. I've been outside."

"And what about your eyes, hmm? What's your brilliant excuse for the size of your pupils?"

"I don't know! Jesus! Ask an eye doctor! I'm not 'on' anything!"

And here, more than a decade later, is the honest truth: I really wasn't on anything! Not that evening, not during that conversation. I have no idea why my eyes looked however they looked to her. But she never did believe me and probably still won't after she reads this, which is fair. I wasn't a very believable person. I spent entire days throwing up because I kept "getting into some bad seafood." I stank of liquor because someone else had spilled some on me, and any crust under my nose was from a persistent summer cold. These were not the alibis of an intelligent schemer. The mess of my life had become a great sucking wound. The pitiful lies I told my mother to cover up my drinking were my attempts to tape the wound shut. I knew it wouldn't heal this way, but maybe at least she couldn't see how deep it went.

My father was the one who first noticed my sloppiness, the same way dogs start acting strange before the humans realize a storm is coming. He'd seen the pandemonium in my bedroom, Barbies and teddy bears strewn all over the floor like the bodies after a massacre. He'd noticed how I stuffed papers into my backpack rather than filing them neatly in my binder the way teachers told us to. One day, he stood mutely at the kitchen counter while I worked at the table, watching me pause every few seconds to play with the dog or gaze longingly at the Tamora Pierce book I wished I was reading.

What he must have been thinking, and what I would eventually realize, is that I came by my chaos honestly. Our two brains had never quite separated from each other, even after I was born, so that he knew everything I was before I did. This played out in all sorts of perfectly mild ways—I cough in the same "voice" that he did, for example, and I'm as unable to keep fuckwords out of my speech as he was. But I'm cracked along all his fault lines, too. Angry like him. Dishonest like him. And now, worst of all in his view: a slob.

He, too, left a trail of destruction in his wake everywhere he went. My mother kept the filth in check when they still lived together, so that I only experienced him as a little disorganized rather than the full-blown disaster animal he became when they got divorced. Then, I could trace his progress across the house by first locating yesterday morning's mug of white-filmed coffee. Underneath it would be a brutalized section of newspaper, its inner guts ripped out and scattered across the floor. I'd follow the tracks those pages made into the kitchen, the centerpiece of which was the mutilated cardboard box from which he'd wrested a frozen pizza. Plus, everywhere, the detritus of cigarettes: stubbed-out butts, empty packs, spent lighters. His house looked like an angry giant's lair, everything broken or torn or discarded.

But that was years later, when my heritage as a slob finally became clear to me. Today, as he watched me fail to do my homework, he was the only one who knew what was waiting for me if I didn't get myself under control.

"Ever wonder how your old man gets any work done?" he asked me.

No, I never had.

"I'm not so organized," he said. "Maybe you've noticed."

Indeed I had—though of course I didn't yet know how euphemistic a designation "not so organized" was.

"The only thing for it is a to-do list." And he showed me his, scribbled near-illegibly in a hand plagued by tremors. The list's dozen items covered an entire sheet of notebook paper. "You're like me. You're not so organized. The only way you're gonna manage is if you write tasks down as soon as you get them, and cross them off as soon as you're done. Get a task, write it down, do a task, cross it off. All day, every day."

I squinted at his list. It was evening, and still only one task was crossed off: *Make to-do list.*

He saw me notice this and yanked the list away again. "Yeah, well. I'm not having such a good day myself."

It turns out I do have ADHD. Well, I'm pretty sure I do—I did originally get that diagnosis by lying to some doctors so I could have my own prescription for Adderall instead of filching my first husband's. But once I began to take treatment seriously, it changed my life. Maybe I accidentally fibbed my way onto a patch of truth. It wouldn't be the first time I told myself something I didn't know I knew, just by lying about it.

I take medicine and, like my not-so-organized father, I have a mania for to-do lists—my husband, Sean, still makes fun of me because I made one for which animals we were going to see at the Bronx Zoo. (It's a huge place! I wanted to make sure we didn't miss the Mouse House!) Thanks to these developments, I can now sit at my desk and begin working when my day starts, instead of what I did for years: scroll numbly through Twitter for hours while berating myself for being such a lazy slob. Maybe most revolutionary of all for me is that I can now actually *listen* to a lecture or speech. My doctor jokes that an inability to focus while listening to a podcast should be a criterion for the disorder, and who am I to argue? She says, too, that ADHD often went undiagnosed for years in girls of my generation because of how often it presents as dreaminess rather than riotousness. If the ADHD Lad is a class clown, the ADHD Gal, like me, is a space cadet.

It's tempting to look at all these improvements and say to myself, phew—problem solved! I was a sloppy, drunken buffoon because I was ill, and, in treating the illness, I have de-slobbed myself. Step aside, Rhodes scholars and MacArthur geniuses! Rax King is here, and she no longer leaves a pan of instant ramen boiling away on the stove for forty minutes because she keeps getting distracted by *The Price Is Right*.

But of course, if I flush my pills down the toilet and set my to-do lists on fire, I slob out again within the hour. If anything, it feels much worse now on the rare occasion that I forget Sean's birthday or allow an old Arizona iced tea can to grow mold on my desk, because I finally share my teachers' and employers' opinion that I'm better than this. *Am* I better than sloppiness on some inherent, inarguable level? Signs point to no. Sloppiness is who I am as much as asthma, and I take medicine for both. I'll never fix my brain—all I can do is recognize what it does well and give it as much help as I can for what it does badly.

I'm a bad drinker and a worse cokehead, and so I'm forced to protect my brain from both drugs by avoiding them. That brain is a bad liar, too, and it sure can be an angry sumbitch when it decides to be. Confronted with even a minor stressor, it has the problematic habit of dramatically declaring that it wants to die. And in a decade of restaurant work, it never did learn how to wait tables worth a damn. It would rather smoke a bong and fuck around on the Internet all day.

The red-pen *SLOPPY!*s of years past have, over time, softened into a mumbling chorus of faceless authority figures. It's described me too many times, and in too many contexts, for me to remember who-all said it and why. My work has always been sloppy, says the chorus; my parents did a sloppy job raising me, and no one was surprised when I grew up to be a sloppy drinker. Well, I'm still a mess even after giving up the sloppy drinking. I remain an implacable shoplifter, and I still throw temper tantrums that would better befit a six-year-old. The biggest change is that now, *I'm* the adult in the room. Good luck getting my mother to attend a conference about my behavior now!

Some part of me thinks I should keep setting myself up for failure, that reducing my burden or cutting myself any slack would be dishonorable. Despite the fact that it never changed a thing when the Diannes of the world said "Do your work or else," I say it to myself all the time. I'm my own boss now. If I skip a day of work, nobody else will write this book. Believe me, I keep asking Sam Irby to do it. She's busy. There's only me.

Proud Alcoholic Stock

The first time I ever got blackout drunk, I stabbed somebody.

Oh, lighten up. It was a gentle stabbing. We were sixteen, and my friend Darby was performing that disgusting graphite pencil magic trick that kids did before the advent of Snapchat, clicking the button on the pencil until the lead tip was long enough to drive through the callus of his palm. Over and over he poked as we watched, mesmerized by the foulness of the act. Then—I have no recollection of my crime but multiple witnesses recounted it for me later—I yelled "BOOOOOO-RING!" and snatched the pencil from him and yes, fine, stabbed him a little. Who cares! He pulled most of the lead from his leg that very night. He didn't end up needing a trip to the ER like we thought. It only took a round of antibiotics to stamp out the infection he ended up getting. So what if he has one measly chunk of lead permanently lodged in his thigh! The world is full of far worse injustices than one measly chunk.

In AA meetings, some alcoholics describe their early intoxications with unmistakable relish, those moments when life felt warm and gooey-magic for the first time and they longed to live as these delicious people forever. Not me. Today I can joke about my brief foray into the stabbing arts, but Lord, I *hated* myself when I first heard what I'd done. I was horrified to picture the secret girl who lived inside me, this stabbing fool, less a party animal than a party golem who feared neither socializing nor consequences while her sober self feared both. Yes, I was horrified, but I wasn't surprised. See, this girl—I'd been expecting her.

I come from proud alcoholic stock. Both my parents are recovering addicts—well, maybe not my dad, who is beaucoup dead and has therefore completed the lifelong journey that is recovery. Still, it's what we all share. My family are drunks the way other families are Teamsters or actors.

In other alcoholics' memoirs, there's often some inadvertently braggy talk about denial: "I had *no idea* I was an alcoholic, because how could I have graduated top of my class at Yale Law if I was," or become vice president at Goldman Sachs, or whatever. Notwithstanding my opinion that achievements of this type should really be classified as signs that you *are* an alcoholic, those lofty proclamations weren't true to my own experience. I never didn't know I was a drunk. I knew I would be an alcoholic someday long before my first taste of liquor—hell, before I knew what liquor even was, when I believed my dad who told me the "Spirits" section of the restaurant menu was where ghosts ordered their food from. Thanks to my parents, I dreaded my alcoholic future the way other little girls dread their first period.

When I came on the scene, my dad had been drug- and alcohol-free for years, and my mom for roughly as long as I'd been alive. They didn't make a good couple except in one regard: their obsessive commitment to sobriety. Twelve-step programs were their Paris. Without those programs, they never would have had me, my mother told me once when I was a teenager. She assumed I would respond with gratitude, not realizing that the last thing any angsty teenager wants to hear is that they came *this* close to never having to do this life bullshit.

From the moment I was born, neither of my parents was ever able to relax again, each certain that they'd be the one to personally trigger a lifetime of addiction in me. They were competitive about it: *You think that was bad, I yelled at her in '04 about her slipping grades!* Alcoholism is often genetic, which they knew, but as it turns out, so is obsessing about one's alcoholism.

I noticed that my parents didn't drink as early as I can remember noticing anything, and what's more, I noticed the hell out of their weird rigidity in the face of alcohol. My childhood friends' parents didn't beeline for the bottle when it appeared, salivating and rubbing their hands together, but neither did they cover their glasses with their palms. My parents covered their glasses. They announced, "No, thanks, I don't drink." They wouldn't even allow waiters to hand them wine lists—my mother in particular always reared away from wine lists like a vampire from a crucifix, which was mortifying.

Today, as a self-actualized adult who's been in therapy for (and I don't mean to brag here) nine whole months, I can admire their refusal to play along even when it made others uncomfortable. At the time, all I noticed was that others *were* uncomfortable, and that it was my parents' fault. There's always a momentary devastating silence in a roomful of drinkers when one person announces that they don't drink. I felt that silence bear down on my family and was ashamed. I was the only kid who thought "wine" and "liquor" were curse words until I was eight years old, when I shushed Hunter Mazzarello for saying "the W-word" in class.

My schoolmates' laughter ringing in my ears, I decided the only solution was to project my feelings about my family's oddity onto my parents, where they rightly belonged. "Why don't you ever drink alcohol?" I accused my mother.

She didn't even look up from her book, which was a problem, since I was clearly trying to pick a fight with her and she was acting like this situation didn't call for one. "Because," she said, "I have a problem with it."

"Like Christine?" Christine was our next-door neighbor and we all knew she'd never covered a glass in her life. Some days, I heard her taking out her trash—two or three trips' worth of shrilly clinking empties.

"Like Christine," she agreed, turning a page. "I quit drinking, though. Your father and I both did. God willing, we'll never drink again."

"So you're *not* an alcoholic," I said triumphantly, like *Gotcha!* What she'd said was, of course, recovery gospel—the belief that even after you quit drinking, you're an alcoholic, and will be one for the rest of your life. This was some 101-level shit for her, barely less tedious than the phase I'd left behind just a few years prior, when I'd asked my parents *why why why* about absolutely everything. But for me, taxonomizing my family's weirdness was a matter of life and death, and so I walked away from our conversation less satisfied than ever.

It's not like my friends' parents behaved like a passel of liquored-up boozehounds. Quite the opposite: alcohol was such a nothing to most of them that they could drink and stop drinking with equal ease, or so it appeared from my young vantage point. *That* was what I expected from my parents. They certainly didn't have to get drunk if they didn't want to, I thought generously, but couldn't they at least be casual about alcohol like everyone else? Take Hilary Zilberman's mother—if she cooked a stew with a cup of Merlot, she'd serve the rest of the bottle with dinner. What could be more casual than that? Or Jenny Sebold's parents, who were chic and urbane and had opinions about tasting notes, which struck me as the height of sophistication. Wine was often on their table, a glass or two poured, but that was it. Which made me wonder: *Was* that it? How could drinking be so evil that my parents would dedicate their lives to hiding from it, when I could see right here at my friend's table that it was nothing more than a glass of Chardonnay paired with broiled fish?

"Listen to yourself," my father said. "Eight years old, trying to harass your mother about *wine pairings.*"

"I wouldn't have done Chardonnay with salmon, personally," my mother said mildly, but her face was tight.

They never said a bad word against parents who drank. But if I mentioned Mr. Sebold's wine choice, my mother's lips clenched in a way they didn't when I described the car he drove. My father was more entrenched in his sobriety at the time than she was, and he could casually absorb information about Cab-Savs and electric corkscrews. But my mom had no such poker face, and I soon learned to stop mentioning what my friends' parents were drinking, which is why I concluded that those parents must have been drunks too, because why would she have had a problem with their drinking if it was truly okay?

By the time I turned ten, I had accepted that I was definitely an alcoholic, as was everyone I'd ever loved or would love. The only way forward for any of us was a lifelong commitment to sobriety. I swore that I would cover my own wineglass some-day, no matter how embarrassing it was, and solemnly kept that promise . . . at least, until someone actually offered me a drink.

Addiction remained largely theoretical for me until the day I brought home a permission slip for the D.A.R.E. program. They don't still do D.A.R.E., do they? Kids longed for it all year when I was in fifth grade. We dreamed about D.A.R.E., gossiped about it; everyone, it seemed, had an older brother who swore that the anti-drug presentation had completely rocked his world; D.A.R.E. was the hottest ticket in town. The letters in the acro-nym stood for "Drug Abuse Resistance Education" or, if you were simply too cool for school, "Drugs Are Really Expensive." One older brother claimed that the cops who'd run his D.A.R.E. presentation had brought in a *real live joint* for students to exam-ine! (What could have possibly been the purpose of that? "Look ye now upon the fearsome visage of the beast, should ye do battle with it"?) What really happened in D.A.R.E. was some cops came and helpfully listed all the drugs you'd never heard of, not to give you a shopping list for your bold and glorious future but rather to make you promise never to try them. The whole thing was pretty boring in reality, but we weren't allowed to participate without a signed permission slip, which enhanced its mystique.

There was D.A.R.E., and then there was the anti-drug presentation that preceded it when I brought my father the permission slip. I had hoped to sidestep yet another lecture about alcohol and drugs from my mother by having him sign the thing instead, but he held on to it for days, until we'd almost reached the big day and I had to pester him. (*You think* that's *bad, I almost didn't sign her D.A.R.E. permission slip!*) Before signing, he sat me down across from him on the couch for the full after-school special.

"Whatever they tell you about drugs in that presentation, know this," he said. "You need to be more careful with that stuff than everyone else in your class. Not because it's inherently bad, but because of your mother and me."

This was shocking—not the be-extra-careful stuff, which was merely a riff on the comfortable old tune my parents had been singing all my life, but this business about drugs and alcohol not being inherently bad. I realized for the first time that not every person in the world was an alcoholic. The liquor wasn't bad. *We* were bad.

Then he showed me one of his NA chips, which appealed to the magpie in me who loved county fair ribbons and Girl Scout badges. He explained that some people were sick in a special way, and that the D.A.R.E. officers were going to try to convince us that drugs and alcohol made everyone sick in the same way and should be universally avoided, but it wasn't true, not for most people. Only it *was* true for me, I *should* avoid alcohol and drugs. Why? Because of this dusty old chip, whose function I didn't understand. He used the words "drug addict." He was my father, and yet he used that scary, weighty term to describe himself.

I'd already been attending NA meetings with my father for years, only I had no clue what they were. He didn't hide it from me, but he didn't explain it, either, and my natural lack of interest in adults kept me ignorant. (If my father had written a book on parenting, it would have been titled *Don't Hide It, Just Don't Explain It,* and it would've been an instant bestseller among men who are on a first-name basis with the staff at family court.) When it was the night of his favorite meeting, he set me up on a rocking horse in a dark corner of the big, echoing room while his friends shared what I later learned were anecdotes about cashing their dead parents' social security checks or robbing strangers on the street to finance their drug habits. Afterwards, we'd go to the Tastee Diner, where everyone but me would shower the waitress with NA-guy gallantry. My father's twelve-step buddies were all sweet, dorky old men with about thirty dollars between them. If this was what drug addicts were, what was the problem?

After my dad's talk, I went to the D.A.R.E. presentation feeling deflated. The officers' pulpy descriptions of crack addiction left my classmates agog and frightened, but only managed to embarrass me. I thought, *That's my dad.* I waited for the cops to describe the stage of crack addiction that happens in a church basement next to a rocking horse and immediately precedes egg creams at the Tastee Diner. It never came. Only headaches, paranoia, heart attacks, and death.

Many of my peers did start getting fucked-up pretty early, but they left me out of the loop until I was fourteen, likely because I was such a pill about drinking and drugs. My early promise to Cover My Wineglass Forever had scabbed over with judgment and resentment towards everybody who didn't share my zeal, which was everybody. Religious fervor gave way to curiosity quickly enough in my system, but by then everyone knew better than to offer me a can or a pipe. I had to lie in the puritanical bed I'd made, feeling left out.

Then one day in ninth grade, a couple years before I stabbed Darby, my best friend Trixie invited me to a party in Jenny Colman's basement. Jenny was the coolest one of us nerds—she was the only one with a sibling old enough to buy booze, which lent her a cachet that we all had to grudgingly respect. More importantly, though, I was nursing high-level crushes on about a half dozen boys, all of whom were said to be going to the party. It was decided: we would go, too.

Hours later, teetering vertiginously in Payless pumps and with raccoon masks of drugstore eyeliner blacking out our eyes, we rang Jenny's doorbell. Mrs. Colman ushered us down to the basement, brightly entreating us to "just give a holler" if we should need anything. She was either the most laid-back or the most oblivious mom alive.

I'd been expecting a scene out of one of my beloved teen comedies—a DJ bumping bass-heavy party music, some wasted nebbish puking into a coat closet. But aside from the requisite red Solo cups, there was nothing Amy Heckerling–inflected about Jenny's party. In fact, with more kids mutely looking at the floor than talking to each other, it could have been afternoon detention.

"Jeez," Trixie said under her breath. "Who died?"

But there was alcohol here, and a couple boys I longed to kiss, and I had spent so long layering every lacy camisole I owned for maximum fashion effect. Despite the party's seeming solemnity, I was determined to get my ya-yas out—hell, *one* ya-ya. So I plopped down on the sofa next to my primary crush, Alex Giannis, who promptly and silently handed me a beer.

"Thanks," I said.

"Ever notice how girls always look best when they wear a balanced outfit?" he said in response. "Yours, for example. That's lace, lace, lace."

I blinked. Had he missed a bunch of words on his way to "hello"?

"Don't get me wrong—there's nothing wrong with lace," he continued. "It's sexy. I just think the best thing is to mix it up. You only need one lace shirt, maybe with a sweater, or something suede."

Jesus Christ. The fuse of my crush blew out. I drank three long sips of my beer so I wouldn't have to respond to Alex, marking two important firsts: my first taste of alcohol, and the first time I drank it for the sole reason that I was too uncomfortable to continue the conversation I'd been having.

The taste revolted me. How would I ever force myself to drink enough of this stuff to ruin my life like my parents said I would? I set the can on the table in front of us, feeling only a hint of woozy warmth in my blood while Alex kept looking at me expectantly. I drank again, avoiding his challenging stare. Trixie watched us from a couple feet away, and I had to avoid her eyes too, so that I wouldn't burst out laughing. So I sipped one more time. The warmth and softness spread. Not far—I couldn't make myself drink any more of that repulsive stuff. The feeling wasn't much to go on but it was, it turned out, enough to go on.

I never forgot my father's warning. I just hadn't realized the day I received it how inevitable intoxicants would become. Maybe I could have saved myself, ingratiated myself with the good girls who loved horses and got straight A's. *They* drank nothing rougher than Sierra Mist. I felt uneasy in their company, though. I was way too bad at every kind of math to get straight A's. Plus those girls didn't think that stabbing someone with a graphite pencil was funny, and I just couldn't make a friendship work if the other person couldn't laugh at the horrible shit I did.

So I drank. Heavily. But I never once drank comfortably. Fifteen years of drinking, and every shot—and I mean *every* shot— weighed on me. I went on countless benders, each one trailed by a long, cold shadow. That's not to say I was the only one in my circle who was closely acquainted with the ugly side of getting trashed. A couple of my friends lost friends, relatives, entire childhoods to other people's addiction. If anything, my life was the inverse of those tragedies: I only existed because I hadn't been preemptively lost to alcoholism. *That* was my burden, knowing that, living with it. Stumbling through the world with that fact squatting on my shoulders, whispering in my ear.

It told me terrible things about myself. Every time I got a smidge more intoxicated than I intended, it was because I was a drunk. On the rare occasion that I successfully drank one beer and headed straight home, that was because I was a drunk too, lying to myself about what a drunk I was. Funnily enough, the first time that I ever questioned whether I was an alcoholic— the first time I didn't just plain know for sure—was the day I decided to quit drinking. I mean, being unable to stop drinking is the whole point, and yet there I was, stopping.

The first day of my sobriety, I was hungover. The second day, jubilant. I slayed the beast before it could massacre the townspeople. I rescued the princess.

In twelve-step programs, this phenomenon is called "pink clouding"—the pink cloud being that early euphoria that tells a freshly sober drunk what a great choice they've made and how beautiful life has become now that they've made it. I was familiar with this idea from my parents, resulting in a pink cloud phase of a measly forty-eight hours, *which is a rip-off.*

Post–pink cloud (R.I.P. RAX'S EUPHORIC SOBRIETY, 4/25/22– 4/27/22, WE HARDLY KNEW YA), my first couple clean and sober weeks were dreary in predictable ways. That wasn't the problem. The problem was that I didn't want them to be the same old dreary predictable weeks of sobriety that other quitters have to tolerate. After all, I was certain I was a drunk the entire time I was drinking. Didn't that buy me a little grace from on high?

I no longer had any choice but to actually think my thoughts. It was as if I'd spent nearly two decades with my internal monologue hog-tied and gagged in a windowless room, and now she was free, and was she pissed! My brain caught up to everything she had missed over the years, entire relationships that she'd never signed off on, jobs she never even realized we'd had.

She remembered hungover mornings when she'd tried desperately to wrest control back from my party golem, only to lose it again by nightfall. I was terrorized, constantly, by the very self-consciousness I'd long managed to silence with alcohol and cocaine.

The assumptions I'd made about the sober community—that I understood them intimately, that I'd be ready to join their ranks the day I was drafted—were not true to the way I'd historically treated my relationships with sober friends. I enjoyed their company, but I look back and see that I always foisted the costs of friendship onto them. Picking an activity, confirming a time: these were tasks I only took on myself when the endgame was getting obliterated. If booze was on my to-do list, my tolerance for social administrative drudgery was bottomless. I never had the same enthusiasm for hanging out in a substance-free capacity. I would wait for my sober friends to invite me places, which they did a couple times a year, and I'd show up and drink soda and stay for a maximum of one hour no matter the activity. A meal, a movie night, bowling, it made no difference. One hour. The rest of the year, I sidelined them from my daily life, which was for partying.

Newly sober, *I* became the sidelined friend. At first, my party pals invited me out as if nothing had changed, and I showed up, pretending nothing had changed. I haggled with myself beforehand: I wouldn't take part in a weekend activity, when people were more likely to be extra wasted. I wouldn't go to a party or dinner that started after 9 P.M.; I wouldn't set foot in any bar I associated with doing coke. There were many rules.

I obeyed them, but the rest of the world did not. I assumed

I'd be safe at my friend Marnie's birthday party, which was scheduled to begin at 7 P.M. on a Monday. How hard could it be to follow all my rules at 7 P.M. on a Monday?

When I arrived, I didn't see Marnie anywhere. So my husband Sean and I posted up in a corner with a couple of seltzer-and-bitters to wait. Nobody likes seltzer-and-bitters. The only good thing about that combination is the liquor your bartender adds to it. Clearly, I was setting myself up for a shitty night from the jump.

Suddenly, Marnie and two other people shot out of the bathroom together in a gale of chattering excitement, and I felt my hackles rise.

"Oh, my *God,*" she gushed, hugging my stiff body. "Thank you *so much* for coming. I know it's not easy for you."

That was to be a theme of my early sobriety: other people's showboating gratitude towards me for coming out. They meant it kindly but, as everything about sobriety set my teeth on edge, I couldn't receive it kindly. All I ever heard was *What a brave and self-sacrificing little wastoid you are.*

But it was Marnie's birthday after all, and she wasn't a self-important sober person. Why shouldn't she do a few bumps at 7 P.M. on a Monday? So in response, I bared my teeth in a smile like an aggressive baboon's.

The night was a disaster. I ordered more seltzer-and-bitters and seethed into my insipid bubbles. I couldn't decide how to stand or arrange my face, two decisions that cocaine had historically made for me. My friends went to the bathroom too often and talked too fast and listened too excitably, just like—it pained me to think it—just like I once did. They smashed beer cans, their breaths stank of yeast. Everything reminded me of my party golem, who whispered seductively from deep inside me. It would have been so easy to rejoin them. I told Sean to go ahead and drink, not to worry about me, I was fine. He did drink and I wasn't fine. Maybe it wasn't even a full hour that I stayed this time. Sober, I was a bad sport.

My father, that proud alcoholic stock from which I come, died from addiction. Not to his old friends alcohol and cocaine, but to cigarettes, the vice they don't count against you when it's time to collect your chip. If he hadn't spent decades laying waste to his lungs, he almost certainly would have survived the fall that ultimately killed him. That might sound like a pretty miserable fact, that he crushed every addiction he could and still died of it, but it actually makes me feel better—how giving up a drug or two does not necessarily entail committing to a good clean life forever. Who knows? Maybe addiction will find a way to kill me, too. One day at a time, as they say.

Growing up with hypervigilant ex-addicts for parents, I thought I could see my doom coming for me. I avoided it as long as I could and then, when avoiding it was no longer possible, I embraced it in a spirit of merry nihilism. When *that* became impossible—when I had to give up the same things my parents did—the nihilism fermented into fear, which is just a feeling of doom without the acceptance. No longer anesthetized against terror, I now had several years of it to triage and process. Now it comforts me to remember that the doom never leaves you, that it gets everyone in the end, whether they've spent their life obsessing over it or not. All I can do is take care of myself moment to moment, in the hopes that on the day I leave this planet, I will have done the best I could.

Well, I can't say I'm doing the best I can, at least not right now. I don't go to meetings, I smoke weed, and I occasionally ponder whether I was ever a real alcoholic or if my anxiety and self-obsession talked me into self-diagnosing unnecessarily. In twelve-step parlance, I'm white-knuckling my way through getting clean. Going it alone, through gritted teeth. I am still in early sobriety, and it still blows.

When I experience this doubt, I remind myself of that first blackout when I stabbed my friend. How it felt to learn that I was capable of damaging someone I loved in a real way, even as I pretended it wasn't the "real" me who had done it. I've stopped thinking of my party golem as an evil alter ego who does things I would never do. She lives in me, I am her home. She counts too. My task is to learn what her problem is and help her heal. I sit and reflect on the backward, ugly ways she believed she was helping me over the years. I listen to what she has to say: *Feed me; I want.* We both need feeding—now it's time for us to learn together what's safe to eat.

Shoplifting from Brandy Melville

The Brandy Melville cashier tells the teenage girls at her register that she can only take exact change for their eighteen-dollar purchase, since she doesn't have any ones in her drawer.

"You can keep the change," says one of the girls, trying to hand over a twenty.

"I can't," says the cashier, visibly bored of this conversation already. "It'll throw off my drawer. Sorry."

The girls eye each other uncertainly and then head for the exit empty-handed, looking dejected and embarrassed. It's time for me to save the day. "If you want to give me the twenty, I can put the dress on my credit card," I offer.

One of the girls turns to me with a grateful, beatific smile. "Would you really?"

"Of course," I say, shifting my purse so I can pull out my credit card without giving the cashier a view of the five tank tops I've stuffed in there. "No sweat."

As it turns out, it is ludicrously easy to shoplift from Brandy Melville. Or maybe it only is for me, because unlike the store's primary clientele, I am in my thirties and therefore invisible.

I probably don't even need to stop at shoplifting. I could run naked through my local Brandy Melville outpost or fling Molotov cocktails through the windows.

I'm at Brandy Melville because I like how clingy and lightweight their tank tops are, and I'm shoplifting from them because I don't drink or do blow anymore. You sort of have to do something, don't you? I still smoke weed, but if anything, that's opposite-partying. The intoxicants I gave up made me unpredictable and dangerous; weed makes me docile, lazy, and *very* receptive to the virtues of snack foods. I haven't explicitly given up acid or molly, but those are both two-day commitments, minimum. After thirty, who has the time? So it's come to this: me benevolently buying these girls a sundress, basking in their gratitude while my purse overflows with Brandy Melville merchandise.

I shoplifted a lot throughout high school, before those clunky security tags were so widespread, when stealing clothes was a more elegant venture. Those damn tags have sucked all the joy and spontaneity out of shoplifting. The enterprising thief now has to remove them with pliers or a magnet, two things that are a real drag to shlep around, especially if a cop finds them in your purse and decides they constitute probable cause. Otherwise, you can cut the tag off in the dressing room with nail scissors and try to convince yourself that your new dress is *more* fashionable with a raggedy hole in it. Shoplifting used to be a battle of wits between me and a store's employees, and I like to think they got as much out of our Tom and Jerry shenanigans as I did.

I wasn't one of those kids who turned her shoplifting into a trade, like Alanna Novak in my tenth-grade class. Alanna stole for the purpose of selling her bounty, and by the time we were fifteen she was already a seasoned merchant who stole only things that would command a high price among her customers— meaning hot-ticket items like limited-edition sneakers and first-generation iPods. She stole much higher-stakes stuff than I ever dared to, and to this day I have no idea how she did it so regularly or in such great quantities.

At lunch, Alanna would take orders in her beloved Lisa Frank pocket notebook that she carried around for this purpose, putting her purple gel pen behind her ear when she was done. She was appealingly animated during her sales pitches, her patter as rapid and slick as an auctioneer's. After school, she'd escort the day's customers to Rock Creek Park where she kept her "shop," which was a sort of lean-to made from a tarp that hid her two chained-up suitcases of loot. It was said that she was part of a whole shoplifting operation with her brother and his friends at college, and that they took a hefty cut of the money she made. But anyone could see that it wasn't about the money for Alanna. She had a knack for sales even at that early age, and if she hadn't had two suitcases of loot to hawk in the woods, she would've happily hustled us for something else. I never bought anything from her, but I was always glad to see her around.

Then one day, I was at the mall with my mother. I had nearly convinced her of the wisdom of buying me an eighty-dollar pair of Tripp pants so heavy I couldn't walk in them when I saw Alanna. And she wasn't alone. Two undercover loss prevention guys from an anchoring department store had nabbed her. One of them held her Lisa Frank notebook aloft, waving it at her like a zealot with a Bible.

I watched her for a few minutes. In school, I barely spoke to her, but I admired her—she was one of those precocious kids who isn't particularly good at school or sports, but excels by virtue of seeming coolly older than her years, maybe thanks to the influence of the mysterious older brother. Now, though, with her eyes cast down and her hands clasped behind her back, she just seemed . . . scolded. Little, and afraid.

My mother watched me watch Alanna. "Friend of yours?" she asked warily. Alanna wasn't the sort of girl that moms encouraged their kids to be friends with.

Somehow, though her lids were low and I had no idea whether she'd even seen me, Alanna seemed to be making eye contact with me. Begging me for something I didn't have.

"Just a girl from school," I said, and hastily jammed the Tripp pants back on the rack. In that moment, I couldn't do anything meaningful for Alanna. But I could at least refuse to dishonor her by buying something with legal tender while the pigs took her down.

Last I heard, Alanna had joined a cult deep in the woods somewhere—not a *really* awful cult I don't think, a camping cult more than a sex or murder one, but it was still sad to hear. I look back at the days when her business was at its peak, her glowing smile and flawless negotiation tactics, and think about how much promise she had.

I don't want to give the impression that I was a pathological shoplifter. I think my old hobby is pretty common among teenage girls, actually—maybe it's a function of all that *stuff* being marketed to us constantly, stuff we don't have the income to buy and only get piecemeal from parents on birthdays and

Hanukkah. It's possible that fast-fashion outlets like Shein and, for that matter, Brandy Melville have relieved girls of their kleptomania, but fifteen years ago, a gal couldn't get a big haul of trendy separates delivered to her door on the cheap. She had to get creative, and a little illegal. When I got my first job at Starbucks, I declared that I was hanging up my extra-big tote bag for good. Well, more or less for good. Certain things I still stole as a matter of principle, like Burt's Bees lip balm. I don't know how Burt's Bees stays in business, because I'm certain that no person has ever actually purchased one of their products. They're all palm-sized, they all beg to be snatched. I hate to say anyone's asking for it, but Burt's Bees is for sure asking for it.

Okay, so I kept the tip of my finger in the pie, but mostly it felt grown-up and luxurious having my own money to buy some of the stuff I longed for every single second. The same inner void I'd eventually fill with drugs could be just as easily packed with stuff. In those years D.C. had some really great shopping, all of which is long gone. There was Commander Salamander, with its punk rock clothes at yuppie prices; here, I could only afford to shop once or twice a year, though I was ideologically loyal to the place and bought my Special Effects hair dye there. But the same people who owned Commander's also owned Up Against the Wall, a much cheaper wonderland overflowing with so many clothes that most of them were stuffed—where else?—up against the store's high walls, all the way to the ceiling. Staff members with extraordinary hand-eye coordination had to use long poles to take individual pieces down. In the time I worked at Starbucks, I'd estimate that a solid 50 percent of my income was tithed directly to the good people of Up Against the Wall.

I spent just as recklessly at Annie Creamcheese, and when I couldn't afford to spend, I took. Even after I gave up my life of crime, I just couldn't resist, like a teenybopper Al Pacino: *Just when I thought I was out . . . !* Annie Creamcheese was a primitive punkish version of the Buffalo Exchanges and Uptown Cheapskates that now plague every corner of every commercial neighborhood. Its two locations were in D.C.'s Georgetown and Las Vegas, the two most opposite places in the country. Evidently, its owners liked extremes. Its sign, a stylized cartoon image of owner Annie Lee blowing a kiss with hot pink lips, drew me in with promises that this wasn't just another Georgetown prep-fest.

Spellbound, I walked down the stairs that led to a black-and-magenta-walled Valhalla. It was a miracle mishmash of consignment goods: rows of jewel-toned cowboy boots marching up to a glass case full of glittering Lucite heels; oversized '70s band T-shirts filed alongside sequined '80s prom dresses with shoulder pads as thick as dish sponges; enamel earrings so heavy they stretched out your lobe holes every time you put them in. A pair of high-waisted jeans with DONNA SUMMER airbrushed across the ass! A necklace with drippy white beads designed to look like a cum shot! Everywhere I looked, I saw wonderful, magical *stuff,* stuff I'd never even dared to imagine could exist, stuff I could rarely afford but always needed to own. What choice did I have?

It was simple: I wasn't addicted to shoplifting. I was addicted to stuff, and shoplifting was the risky thing I had to do to stave off the DT's.

———

I got caught only once.

It was at the beginning of my freshman year of college, which is an embarrassing time to get caught shoplifting, not least because you're eighteen now and can be fined or even tried like any other adult crimester. My friends and I had just met at freshman orientation a few weeks prior, and now we were embarking on a panty-snatching mission in the same spirit in which other girls might play Two Truths and a Lie.

In Annapolis, where we attended school, getting to the mall with all the good shoplifting was no easy matter. I was used to D.C.'s robust public transit system, but when I asked a fellow student about the bus to the Annapolis mall, he laughed in my face. "Yeah, I know that bus," he said. "It runs about once every twelve days." This unreliability turned our game into a high-stakes odyssey: we had no idea how long it would really take us to get where we were going, and knew we might have to wait an hour or more for our getaway driver. We'd been giggly and buoyant when we left the dorms, but by the time we arrived at the mall, all three of us were tired and cranky and ready to go home. What I'm saying is, I blame the piss-poor quality of public transit in Annapolis for the careless way we shoplifted that day.

All three of us stuffed 5-for-25 thongs in our purses in muted determination, peering up occasionally at the ceiling mirrors to make sure nobody was watching us, which of course is the fastest way to get security staff to watch you. But one of us let her guard down, snatching one thong too many on the wrong side of the store and failing to notice the undercover loss prevention guy in his backwards baseball cap. (I dearly love how every rent-a-cop everywhere thinks a backwards baseball cap is a slick disguise. It's barely a step up from one of those Groucho Marx mustache/glasses things you get at Party City!)

We regrouped silently and left together, only to hear what every shoplifter dreads hearing: "Excuse me! Miss! Stop right there!" Later, I confirmed that all three of us had the same thought: *What would happen if we ran?* But we knew what would happen—we'd run as far as the bus stop fifty feet away and then get stuck waiting for God knows how long. So we turned, accepting our fate.

I wasn't technically the one who got caught, so actually, I've been caught zero times. By that I mean we were all together, but the loss prevention guy had only seen my friend Greta in the act, so she was the only one he could apprehend—one common guideline among shoplifters is that loss prevention staff are technically only supposed to nab a thief they've watched steal and leave the store, lest they be guilty of crying wolf and making the store vulnerable to a lawsuit. (Why does the thief have to leave the store? Because if Johnny Loss Prevention stops her before she does, she can claim she was still planning to pay, making Johnny guilty of crying wolf and the store vulnerable, again, to a lawsuit.) (I didn't have to research any of this stuff, by the way. It lives as deep in my memory as my childhood phone number. In middle school, when they split up the boys and girls for health class, the boys learn about boners and semen and whatnot and the girls memorize various department stores' loss prevention manuals.)

Anyway, it was a lot like that day in the mall with my mom

and Alanna. The LP guy removed his backwards baseball cap, neutralizing his disguise, and instructed Greta to hand over her haul. Then he asked me and my other friend, Liz, if we'd taken anything. We lied that we had not, and of course he knew we were lying, but what could he do? He hadn't been watching us two. So he contented himself with taking Greta away for further questioning.

"What do we do now?" Liz asked.

"Wait, I guess," I said. From where we were standing, I could see the next bus home pulling into the parking lot.

We did wait—I don't know how long. I suggested at one point that we distract ourselves with some window shopping rather than just stand there looking all dead-man-walking, but Liz noted that we had purses full of stolen underwear and should probably limit our exposure to other stores' loss prevention staff. So we kept standing there, dejectedly pointing out the departing buses to each other, until Greta came back out with a look of grim resignation on her face.

"Ladies, shall we?" she asked, and we agreed that we should.

Greta told us later what every shoplifter wants to know, which is what actually happens when you get taken in hand as a thief. It seems Officer Baseball Cap took her into a scuzzy little room, a carbuncle on the ass of the department store, and made her fill out some basic paperwork—name, address, and so on. He and a colleague told Greta that she could never come back to this mall, or she would face even worse consequences. Then they took her picture.

That last part intrigued me. "So you're going to be on, like, a real WANTED poster?"

"I don't know what they do with the picture," she said. "I didn't see WANTED posters on the walls or anything."

"Maybe it's just to scare you off coming back to the mall," I suggested. "Like, just knowing that they know what you look like . . ."

Later, feeling guilty that I hadn't gotten caught like she had, I gave her one of the thongs I'd stolen.

"One last haul," she said with a rueful grin.

The adrenaline rush, the full-body tingle of walking through a store's door with illicit goodies in my purse . . . those pleasures are real, and they do count towards the overall fun of any shop-lifting project. Really, though, I shoplift the way the proverbial middle-class housewife pops an Ativan at 2 P.M. or has one glass too many at bottomless brunch. I'm a domesticated animal. This is the wildest behavior that's available to me now.

I'm not one of those noble and downtrodden people you hear about who have no choice but to shoplift the food they can't afford to buy for their loved ones. Anyone with a conscience can agree that such people have a moral imperative to steal, and that when they face consequences for doing so, it's unjust. But even I think it would be just for me to face *some* consequences for shop-lifting. I steal for no reason, and I'm smug and annoying about it. When I pull it off, I tell my friends excitedly about the crime I just committed, a behavior that my public-defender father once told me is how nearly all his clients got caught. Maybe it'll all catch up with me someday, but that's a problem for future Rax. In the meantime, Brandy Melville is the methadone clinic weaning me off sin, its gloriously untagged merchandise my synthetic high.

Pants on Fire

"Anne Shirley, do you mean to tell me you believe all that wicked nonsense of your own imagination?"

"Not believe *exactly*," faltered Anne. "At least, I don't believe it in daylight."

—Lucy Maud Montgomery, *Anne of Green Gables*

When I was twelve years old, I learned by accident that my father had three ex-wives.

I'd assumed until then that he'd only ever been married to my mother, to whom he was still married at the time. (By the end of his life, he would have *four* ex-wives.) As a child, when one of your parents doesn't explicitly tell you he's been married a whole mess of times, you don't assume he's hiding something. But that day, we were at the home of a man in his late thirties named John David Jr., whom I naively believed was a family friend. His sister Margaret was there, too, and their mother Margaret, the two of them known respectively as Little Maggie and Big Maggie. Big Maggie's ex-husband, John David Sr., was not there. (Catholics, my God, is this stuff really necessary? Some of us have assaulted our brains with drugs for too long to keep your names straight anymore.)

I'd known these people all my life without paying them much attention. After all, my parents were always shlepping me from place to place so that I could "visit" with their boring grown-up friends. That was how my mother, especially, phrased it: "Rax, put down that book and come visit with your grandmother!" The only notable thing about visiting with the Maggies and John Davids was that my father and I always did so alone—no mother in tow. About this, I'd never asked questions. It made perfect sense to me that she wanted to avoid these catastrophically dull get-togethers, where no one had the decency to show any interest in the things I liked because they had to talk for five hours about their mortgages. I wanted to avoid them myself.

So there I was, wretched with the boredom that comes with being the only child in the room, when the talk turned to learning to drive. That's when Junior gave me a mischievous look. "You know," he said conspiratorially, "your dad's just about the best driving teacher there is. It only took him a few days to teach me everything I needed to know back when he lived with us."

I blinked. The Catholics beamed at me. My father stared out the window in a determined pantomime of not paying attention.

"I think my dad might have said something to me about that once," I said lamely, and it felt gross, like I was covering for him.

Now I knew: Big Maggie was not just a family friend, but my father's third ex-wife. Little Maggie and Junior were his stepkids. Maybe I should have put together that he was roughly parent-aged in relation to them, that the four of them had always been a smidge cozier than was typically warranted by a family friend relationship. I suppose I should have noticed, too, the photos on Big Maggie's mantelpiece that showed her and my father together—but then again, *should* I have noticed? I was *twelve*. The only thing I could be counted on to notice was whether the cute guy in my social studies class was playing pickup on shirts or skins that day.

Years later, I got the full catalogue of ex-wives. There was Barbara, his law school classmate; my grandmother learned that the two of them were living together and demanded they marry at once, lest she (my bubbe) die of shame. Velma was next in line, a slender wisp of a TV actress who spoke with a spurious British accent. After Velma came Big Maggie, whom I knew; and after her came my mother. My aunt Esther suggested that he'd never told me about these women until he had no choice because he didn't want me to think of him as "that kind of guy"—the four-wives kind, I suppose. That might not have been so bad if the women weren't in his life anymore, but I'd been visiting his ex-wife and stepkids for years, and the whole time he'd deliberately hidden who they were!

My father would feebly protest over the years that he hadn't been deceitful. "You never asked," he pointed out. "If you had asked, I would have told you."

"Well, it's not the sort of thing you usually have to *ask*, is it?" I said. "What would I have even said? 'Dad, weird question, but have you by any chance been married four times?'"

Knowing he was licked, my dad performed the last-ditch defense of the cornered Jewish parent: guilt. "Maybe, if you had ever shown the slightest bit of interest in your old dad's life before you came into it, you would have learned a thing or two."

He was full of shit and we both knew it. The more plausible explanation was that my father had never lost the slippery addict's habit of not-quite-lying while still, you know, *lying*. Even about low-stakes stuff, even when the person most inconvenienced by the lie was him. What mattered most was the power his lies gave him to construct his own reality, one where his relationships with women were less dysfunctional and his only problem with his daughter was that she needed to show more interest in him. He managed to live in that reality until he died. I'm still dismantling it to this day.

I'm not unsympathetic to a person's need to live in a fake world, though. The real world isn't easy. You've got to fill out so many forms and remember whether you've taken your pills, and the best-case scenario is a long slow rot off the earth. I don't blame my father for believing he had the power to construct a brighter version of it all. I believed it about myself once, too.

Yes, I used to be quite the little fabulist. I don't think I ever meant to mislead, exactly, though of course that's exactly what my lies did. But all I ever wanted as a girl was to punch up the dull first draft that was reality. I'd discovered a loophole: I could become everything I'd ever dreamed of being, all without working for it. All I had to do was say the words.

One evening when I was eight, I caught a few minutes of a show about professional magicians and took a fancy to the performers' skill and dexterity, neither of which were traits I'd exhibited thus far in my young life. It was the perfect use case for a lie: I could try on a magician's life without the commitment of a magician's education, which the show had indicated was arduous and took many years. "Arduous" and "takes many years" wouldn't do me much good on the playground. Instead, during the next day's routine session of double Dutching and Miss Mary Macking with my friends, I simply told them all that I could bend spoons with my mind.

Most of the girls oohed and aahed appropriately, but my friend Rachel looked dubious.

"No way," she said hesitantly.

"I can so," I said, emboldened by her uncertainty. "I learned I could do it and now I do it all the time, practically. It's a power some people have."

The next day, Rachel's mom picked me up for our carpool to school, a soup spoon in her hand. "I'm just *dying* to see your powers," she told me. Rachel wouldn't look at me.

I took the spoon, frantically trying to figure out a last-minute trick I could play to convince Rachel and her mother that I'd really bent it. But there, that was exactly the problem. If I'd known such a trick, the lie wouldn't have been a lie in the first place.

I remember this, though: up until the last second, when the spoon remained rigid and I had to apologize for telling stories, I believed the whole thing would work itself out. I reckoned that the spoon would decide of its own accord to help me, or that this would be the moment I learned I really could bend spoons with my mind. I didn't have the skill of telling believable lies. What I had instead was this perverse, optimistic conviction that the lies I told, once I told them, became true.

———————

Even a liar who only intends to brighten up her surroundings can't always resist the temptation to use her powers for evil. As a kid, I mostly lied because I had such glorious visions for what my life could have been—the beautiful name I wished my parents had given me (Antoinette, which, in retrospect, *ew*), the fascinating careers my parents might have had. If I simply claimed those visions were the reality, I fancied, other people would fall in line on their own. It was as innocent as wrongdoing can be until it became a habit. My lies started off as a rich dessert that I could only gorge myself on once a week, but by the time I was a teenager, I was snacking on them as mindlessly as I would have an open bag of Cheez-Its.

My specialty was the lie so dastardly that authority figures had to pretend to believe it. If my teachers had ever cross-referenced my excuses for not doing homework, they would have uncovered about twelve grandmothers, each the victim of a more baroque death than the last. I did dead grandmothers the way Nic Cage does screams: with such gusto that their frequent implausibility was all part of the fun. There were car crashes, rare illnesses. Electrical fires and tragically preventable swimming pool accidents. One grandmother overdosed on heroin at the Joshua Tree Inn à la Gram Parsons—you know, the sort of thing that might befall any grandmother. Not once did any of my teachers dare to point out that most people's nanas go much gentler into that good night.

Lies of convenience still weren't my primary game, even as I told them more and more often. It was intoxicating, though, how no one had the balls to call me out. I suppose we were all just trying to get through the drudgery of daily life—me by painting over it with colorful unreality, my teachers by pretending to ignore the offensive graffiti that resulted.

But I came to miss the days when each lie was a precious thing, crafted and tended with care. When I debased my hobby by lying about my unfinished homework or whether I'd been smoking cigarettes with my friends, it felt like stepping into someone else's sweat-soaked socks, a bad and dirty fit. Grandmother-and-cigarettes lies were for amateurs (who can't think of anything more exciting to be dishonest about) and scumbags (who don't care enough about being trusted to lie well). I didn't like lying to save my own ass. I wanted to return to the nobility of big lies that nobody believed.

In the days before my many dead grandmothers bought me passes on my incomplete homework, the lies I told, like my dad's, actually made my life harder. They required research and mental contortions that even the most dedicated meditation practitioner would have found challenging. Was I an understudy for an opera singer at the Kennedy Center today, or would this be the day when my parents were taking me to the DMV after school to change my name, finally, to Antoinette? (Again: *ew.*) You could track my education through my lies: I had just learned about opera, or the Kennedy Center, or the DMV, or a certain French queen. Today, I'm forced to incorporate anything I learn into my writing instead, which at least is a form of bullshit that people will pay you for.

Lies of convenience asked their listeners to adjust their behavior: *Hear my tale, good lady, and grant me an extension on this paper as a result of it.* Such falsehoods didn't just throw glitter over the image I wanted people to have of me. They altered the real conditions of my life. They won me unfair advantages. They were still magic, but now they were black magic, evil rather than silly.

My dishonesty plateaued when I was married to my first husband . . . Oh, you can't imagine how chic it feels to casually mention my *first* husband. Picture me smoking a cigarette out of a long holder while I say it, wearing a fascinator hat. I don't know why my dad wanted to rob himself of this experience by lying to me for twelve years about his marriages, when it's just as chic for men. Anyway, when I was married to my first husband, I cheated on him like you wouldn't believe.

I slept with other men and women because it was Tuesday or because the Ravens had won the Super Bowl. Not the whole time we were together, mind you. At first I was faithful, obsessively so. It only took a few weeks of marriage to realize what a disaster we were, but our horny animal selves cherished each other, and so I embraced fidelity as the only available sign that our relationship might not be all bad.

Then I began to notice the unusual attention he paid his friend Kimberly, who sold us heroin sometimes. No matter how many people were in the room, he found a way to end up next to her; whenever he stumbled into our apartment at four in the morning, it was her house he was stumbling in from. And as soon as I noticed it, it exploded into an emotional affair that I couldn't ignore. He wouldn't admit that he was cheating on me, first because he hadn't had sex with her and later, once he had, because he'd gotten too used to the benefits of life in the alternate reality where he was a faithful husband. He was a liar, too. Maybe we were a good match after all.

I knew he hadn't slept with Kimberly yet and also that I couldn't stop it from happening; it felt important, at least, to beat him to the punch. So I had sex with our weed dealer, Nate. My husband had conquered vast swaths of me in that marriage and then, just when I was on the verge of total surrender, he abandoned his claim in favor of conquering new terrain. Cheating was my sneaky rearguard maneuver. The enemy was busy invading elsewhere, and I saw an opportunity for a little defense. While my husband courted the dope dealer, I slept with the weed dealer. It struck me as poetic—a wartime symmetry.

I wasn't certain about my prospects with Nate at first. Yes, he seemed attracted to me, but I had met him through my husband, who adored him. Every other sentence out of his mouth began with a worshipful "Nate says" or "Nate thinks." In truth, I found most of the things Nate said and thought fairly stupefying. He had a penchant for making libertarian Joker memes, a sentence that I detest having to write about a man I've known biblically. But he was cute and there, so. I've fallen in love on less.

I worried that my then-husband's adoration might be mutual enough for Nate to reject me under the auspices of bro code. So I sidestepped the issue. I made an appointment to buy weed, to which I wore three competing perfumes and no panties. I figured I'd find a way to casually (and dishonestly) mention that my husband and I sometimes dated other people. I hadn't considered that as soon as I arrived, Nate would set the course of conversation, as he always did, on an express trip straight to Conspiracy Theory Junction, where he held me hostage for several minutes, projecting various close-up images of dollar bills onto his wall and explaining each one's significance to the NSA. Weed may not have been the only thing he'd been smoking that day.

He had no air-conditioning, and I could feel the raw poultry slickness of my freshly shaved legs and crotch all melding under my skirt. How many more pictures of triangles would I have to look at? How long did I have before my sweat started to stink? There was no time to lose.

"My husband and I have been into dating other people lately," I said, seizing on the moment's silence that had set in while he searched his hard drive for the next slide.

"Word," Nate said, and immediately lunged at me with a kiss, as if I'd just used his activation phrase.

We fucked. It was pretty good.

"One thing," I said afterwards as we lay in his bed, each of us smoking a joint that only a true craftsman could have rolled. The benefits of sleeping with the weed man. "Don't tell my husband about this next time you see him. We have sort of a don't-ask-don't-tell arrangement."

A beat of silence, a heaviness leaching into the air.

"If you say so," Nate said. He didn't believe me. What he believed was that it was in his interests not to call me out.

I slept with Nate in large part so I'd have something on my husband, a single victory brightening up a vast dark landscape of defeats and humiliations. Infidelity was the only area where *I* was a step ahead of *him,* and having overtaken him, I thought I'd be able to relax. I didn't understand how addictive it would be, pulling one over on a man who took for granted that he could always outmaneuver me.

After Nate, there was no one else for a long time . . . well, for a few weeks anyway, but that's a long time in abusive-husband years. At first, my infidelity had made me more kindly disposed towards him. When he belittled my looks or my cooking now, I smiled, the very picture of wifely submission, while thinking *You have no idea that I have had your buddy's cock inside me.* I could gratify my husband by behaving as if he'd broken me, my catastrophic secret dangling over his head all the while like the blade of a guillotine. I figured I only needed the one secret to dangle.

But one night, I was at our local dive, where I'd been waiting nearly an hour for him to join me. I was drinking a bourbon at the bar, preparing my opening statement for our imminent fight about how he was always late to meet me after seeing Kimberly, when an unfamiliar man broke my reverie by asking if he could sit next to me. I took in his drowsy gray eyes and the gold chain nestled into a tempting thicket of chest hair and said he certainly could. I felt obligated to add that my husband would be arriving any minute.

"Tell ya one thing," the man said with a grin. "If you were *my* wife, I sure wouldn't be leaving you alone in a place like this to raise hell."

How I missed being seen as a sexy troublemaker! Most days it felt like my husband didn't see me at all, but when he did, it was as an obstacle or a stooge. *His* role was to make trouble, while mine was to wait for his return—preferably patiently, but he didn't mind when I picked fights, either. What mattered was that he remained the protagonist, the prime mover.

It had been some time since a hot stranger had plied me with clichés, but I still knew all my lines. "Am I raising so much hell?"

"No," he said. "You're fine. Those legs are what's raising hell."

That was the moment, an hour late and in no visible hurry, when the prime mover chose to show up. The stranger respectfully turned away, the loss of his attention like a cloud blocking the sun. My husband grabbed the stool on my other side and squeezed my calf under the bar by way of greeting. I was now sandwiched between the devil I knew and the devil I didn't.

"Sorry I'm late, babe," he said, scanning the menu. "Traffic coming back from Kim's was awful."

I'd been preparing a snide response to exactly that, something about how *funny* it was that traffic was always *so* awful on the way back from Kimberly's house. But I was distracted just then by the fingers crawling lazily up my other calf. My husband's hand on me was perfunctory; this one was hot and knowing and determined. It felt like it was trying to find its way in the dark, stroking every contour of my leg as it climbed. I stole a peek at the stranger beside me. His eyes pointed straight ahead in a believably uninterested thousand-yard stare. No shadow of a smirk, no wink gave him away. No one but me knew what was going on under the bar.

My husband gushed about all the fun he'd just had at Kimberly's while I tried to feed him just enough "oh yeah?"s and "wows" to convince him I was listening. He really should have noticed something was up—I never tolerated conversations about Kimberly's incomparable perfection for this long. But his crush and his self-absorption kept him oblivious. All the while, his reliable old hand sat on my right leg like a benign growth while the stranger's hand prospected deeper into trouble up my left, dodging my husband's fingers with the smooth confidence of a blockade runner. He didn't stop anywhere for long, didn't seem to be in any hurry. Just meandering across my terrain, cocky and dangerous, brushing across various points of interest with an amused pleasure I could feel, until at length his hand found what it wanted. That's when even my token responses gave way to silence, lest the rapture in my voice betray me and my new friend. My very pleasant, very dear new friend.

My husband let go of my leg and excused himself to use the restroom. The stranger and I finally looked at each other, exhilarated. After all that hypnotic, secretive stroking, the directness of our eye contact nearly knocked me off my barstool. He sucked one finger clean, offered me another. The bartender was gawking at us, but I didn't care.

"You've gotta let me see you again," he said. He seemed like he spent a fair bit of time hitting on women in bars—as a woman who'd spent a fair bit of time hitting on men in bars, I knew and respected my countertype. But feeling up a married woman while her oblivious husband sat next to her was obviously a new frontier for us both.

"You know I can't," I said, sounding like I could and wanted to.

"Look at me and tell me that didn't just turn you the fuck on. Tell me that and I'll leave you alone."

I meant to, I really did. I meant to repeat my self-serving assertion that I had cheated on my husband only once, and only as an act of tactical vengeance. Adding this new man into the mix was indefensible—I would be decadently embracing dishonesty rather than directing it towards a carefully considered purpose, however much I wanted to find out what he could do with *two* hands. But when I looked up at him and tried to plant my feet in what remained of my moral high ground, I saw, in this order: soft lips, lush curls, broad chest, not my husband.

"See?" he said. He chuckled, scribbling his phone number on my receipt. "You can't lie."

One of the hardest things about being sober is this nagging feeling that I'll never use my most powerful skill set again. Like a football star with a career-ending injury, I retired before my time. I'm thirty-three years old and routinely feel this profound, bodily *itch* for actions I can't perform anymore for my own good. God willing, I will never again need to cut perfectly symmetrical lines of powder or spot a junkie house from a block away. That panicked sense of atrophy must drive a good percentage of relapses. It's not like there are that many constructive alternate uses for the ability, which just about all addicts have, to find and efficiently consume drugs anytime, anywhere.

The lying, though, that's a skill I could take to the grave. Only . . . I don't *want* to lie anymore. A big part of sobriety is establishing the ability to sit quietly in the world you've got, not grasp after the unreachable world you want. The imaginary universes built by dishonesty can be all shadows or all light, but the most salient thing about them either way is that they're imaginary. I constructed them, and I can demolish them. I played many roles in the beautiful lie-world I once built for myself, but the constant was that I was always some kind of star or genius. It's the same core need I was chasing with drug use or with cheating on my husband: to be a star, to be a genius. To be anyone other than the mousy crybaby I feared I really was.

That's not to say that I've given up my old pastime completely. Lately I've been workshopping a fun new lie, which is that I know every plot development of every TV show before it happens. The other night, my husband Sean and I were watching Season 3 of *The Marvelous Mrs. Maisel* when the titular comedian Mrs. Maisel went on tour with a singer named Shy Baldwin.

On the show, Shy had a girlfriend he seemed distinctly uninterested in. It was the perfect opening.

"I think he's gay," I announced.

"Huh," Sean said. "What makes you say that?"

"They're clearly setting it up that way," I said, having just covertly read the show's Wikipedia page on the toilet. "I mean, trite much?"

A couple episodes later, the show revealed that Shy was, indeed, gay. Sean elbowed me in the ribs with delight. "You were right! How is it that you can always spot this stuff?"

"Well, I'm a writer," I said. "You learn to keep an eye out for this sort of thing."

It's a relief to only lie about how I know a TV character is gay or a dope fiend or leaving the competition after this episode. I'm now an essentially honest person who gets a little prankish with the truth only when the truth doesn't matter. I no longer lie about where I've been or who I was with, because the answers to those questions are always acceptable now. As for the fun lies, the creative lies . . . there's no point anymore in pretending I just left my shift at the spoon-bending factory to meet my mother at the DMV for a name-change operation. That made-up life doesn't have any space for the people I love. Their parts are being played by glamorous actors who are ultimately useless to me, because they can't crack jokes with me while watching TV on the sofa like Sean can.

These days, I remember my father's face when he was caught with three ex-wives he wasn't supposed to have. That trapped and frightened expression as he tried not to catch my eye—! Did he begin putting together his defense right then, or did he have a bugout bag of excuses ready to go? His sister thought he wanted to protect my image of him, but a subtler deception was at work. At some point, he'd shyly rendered a world he thought seemed nice, where he had always been a devoted husband to his one and only wife. By the time I learned the truth, I'd been living in that world with him my whole life. It was pleasant there, but that shadowy pleasantness was no match for the relief of emerging, squinting, into the sun.

The Temple of Feminine Perfection

My first exposure to the power of hot women was . . . Okay, I might as well admit that it was via the movie *Home Alone 3*. The plot of *Home Alone 3* is that a boy named Alex is home alone and terrorists break into his house to steal his remote control car (?).

Now, I'm not really a *Home Alone* kinda gal. I was too young to partake of early Culkin-mania, and by the time the franchise began gasping its death rattles with the third installment, I hadn't developed the taste for mischief and capers that *Home Alone* fandom requires. But I thought one particular scene was excellent: One of the bad guys is tiptoeing around Alex's house when he hears singing from the bathroom. He creeps in . . . and the singing is coming from a *hot woman*! In the *shower*!

He does what any man would, or at least any man who knows he's in a mischief-and-capers family comedy: opens the shower curtain with a big "don't mind if I do!" grin on his face. Only . . . *No . . . it can't be!* His seducer is just a parrot singing next to a cardboard cutout of a naked babe. The babe in the cutout is arching her back suggestively, the considerable curve of her breast cut off by a carefully placed towel (this is a *family* comedy, remember).

But no, rewind, pause, come on, *pause*—for this was the VHS era, which my friends and I spent rewinding and pausing on the scraps of nudity that benevolent directors tossed into their PG-rated movies. We paused on every individual frame. We looked with eyes that had become mouths. We were all too young to understand what, exactly, the towel was hiding. But it was hiding something; that was enough to make us root against it. We were newly possessed by the urge to *gawk*—not at the world as a team of trustworthy grown-ups had always presented it to us, but at everything we now realized they'd been hiding, hoarding for themselves.

There was no first time I felt attracted to hot men. I came to it gradually, as if from a refreshing sleep. Attraction to hot women was more like sitting bolt upright at 3 A.M., sweating. I looked at that cardboard cutout and awoke from uneasy dreams to discover myself transformed into a giant hard-on. I had never felt mesmerized by a man, no matter how good he looked. I had certainly never *stared* at one.

I learned something about women that day. They had something men didn't; they had something men wanted. Whatever it was, I wanted some of it for myself.

At twenty, I dropped out of college and moved back to D.C.

I needed to find a job, no easy task for me in my blue and dismal state. The same untreated mental illness that had torpedoed my academic performance now wafted off me like a bad smell. I visited the managers at every coffee shop where

I'd worked, however briefly. No dice. They knew they couldn't stick me in front of their customers. Who wants to buy food from a girl who looks and behaves like she's spent the last three months trapped underground?

At a loss, I reached into my pocket to grab a dollar and found exactly that, one lonely dollar, crumpled in the most distant reaches of my pocket like it was hiding from me. A coin was loitering in there, too, so coated in grit as to be indistinguishable from a button. My lackadaisical job hunt crashed over me and broke. I wanted to succumb to the crying jag that had been looming over me all day, but instead I called my stripper friend Liv, who had promised weeks ago that I could come work with her.

She instructed me to meet her at her workplace for an audition that afternoon. "As soon as you can, before it gets busy," she said. "And bring something sexy! You'll only be dancing for one song, so make sure it's easy to take off." Then, a moment's pause while she weighed the wisdom of saying something rude. "And, um, shower."

I looked down at my outfit, which was more or less what any mentally ill twenty-year-old would have worn in 2012 with a dollar and unknown cents or buttons to her name. Fortunately, Liv's strip club wasn't far from home, where I had heels and bras and panties that matched—well, that were all black, at least. I would, um, shower. I would apply makeup, I would approximate a hairstyle. I would silence the scream of desperation that threatened to escape my mouth every minute that I failed to earn a second dollar.

The strip club where Liv worked no longer exists, and appears to have been replaced with a glitzier-looking strip club. But she and I knew it as the King's Castle, a dump squatting across the street from a megahotel for tourists. Other cities do their best to hide their strip clubs. They stick them all on a single grimy block, or bury them behind train tracks. Not D.C., a city whose clubs are scattered all over its limited acreage. Many clubs, including the Castle when it existed, are in otherwise tony neighborhoods whose residents spend every city council meeting begging their public officials to close them down.

The King's Castle duly camouflaged itself to better blend in with its surroundings. It tried to look innocent. Its sign did not say GIRLS GIRLS GIRLS or display neon silhouettes of busty broads. There was only a humble yellow awning, featuring the club's name in delicate red script as well as the vague promise of BAR, FOOD, AND FUN. The sign quieted the neighbors' grumbling, though it did, regrettably, make the club look like a Chinese restaurant from the outside, which led to some confused families walking in for a meal. Many's the twelve-year-old tourist that the bouncers had to shoo away from sneaking back in without his mortified parents.

The sign was confusing, but at least passersby didn't realize there was a big filthy *titty bar* on this good Christian block. I had a hard time realizing it myself. I walked right past the King's Castle four times before the bouncer outside said I was at the right place. He waved me in sans ID when I said I was there to audition—customers have to be twenty-one, dancers don't. That didn't stop Edina, the club's lushly pretty owner, from offering me a shot of whiskey before my audition. "To loosen up," she said with a warm smile, and I, unaccustomed to being served in bars, couldn't resist. Liv was onstage, clapping her ass for the two men in the room at 3 P.M. on a weekday. She and they looked bored.

I waited for Edina to escort me to the private audition room, which I was about to learn didn't exist. "You're next," she said as Liv's song began winding down. "You ready to get up there?"

No privacy, then. That was okay—the whiskey was doing its stuff. I was as ready as I'd ever be. Liv smacked my ass hard for luck as I took the stage, and the DJ put on the song "Rack City."

Rax City, I thought.

My heart drummed in my chest as I danced for those two men, who never looked any less bored. Liv was mouthing something at me from the bar. *Sledding? Slumber?* She scribbled on a cocktail menu and held up her makeshift sign: SLOWER!!!

I powered down to half speed, which made me look less like I was leading a Jazzercise class. One of the men began to look faintly interested. Encouraged, I smiled at him and held his stare as I wiggled out of my bra, then my panties. In offstage life, I struggled to maintain eye contact with anybody, but some long-unused instinct in me was waking up. It told me this was no moment to look away.

Liv and Edina were vigorously thumbs-upping me now.

I was sweating and panting with exhaustion before the song even hit its halfway mark, but the man didn't care. He came to the stage and handed me a ten-dollar bill.

"Thank you," I said, trying not to convey the awe I felt. Ten dollars for two minutes' work was more than I'd ever made.

"Thank *you*," he said, as the song ended. I grabbed my bra

and panties and jogged nude to the bar, with Edina following
me in a panic, shrieking that I had to keep my damn clothes on
when I wasn't onstage.

"Let me taste your drink," said the man I'd been sitting with for
half an hour, and I groaned internally.

"You don't want to do that," I said, trying to maintain my
dirty-girl murmur despite my nerves. True, the bass in the club
always blasted loud enough to rattle the heels of my Pleasers
against the floor, such that my dirty-girl murmur was more
of a dirty-girl holler ("I SAID YOU CAN TUCK THAT DOL-
LAR RIGHT INTO MY GARTER! . . . NO, *TUCK* THAT
DOLLAR!" and so forth). But what did I know from sultry then,
anyway? I was twenty. It was still my first week.

The problem with my drink, which my suspicious customer
had clearly hipped to, was that it contained none of the alcohol he'd paid for. At a normal bar charging normal amounts for
drinks, he might not have paid such Columbo-like attention to
the exact color and smell of my highball glass. But this was a
strip club, and worse, a D.C. strip club. A drink in any strip club
is exorbitantly expensive, but in the District, where a prissy zon-
ing regulation required nude dancers to maintain at least three
feet of distance between themselves and customers at all times,
every cocktail cost as much as a rib eye in a medium-fancy steak-
house. Clubs in D.C. couldn't offer lap dances or champagne
rooms in those years. Like movie theaters, they cashed in on the
concessions.

In reality, I was less a stripper than a daringly dressed cocktail
salesman. When I wasn't dancing onstage, my job was to shake

down my customers for tips and cocktails. The tips were mine to keep, after I tipped out the DJs and waitresses; the cocktails, though, were a pain. I was expected to hustle them hard, but if I'd actually drunk all the liquor I bullied my customers into buying for me, I would've succumbed to cirrhosis. The secret was to have the bartenders make my drinks alcohol-free—a secret because the unspoken engine of the club's success was that these men hoped I'd get drunk enough to make some error of judgment with them. That was why they were willing to pay so much for a drink. At least when you pay nine dollars for a soda at a movie theater, you get the soda.

That's why this guy had been so sour and suspicious the entire time I'd been sitting with him. I'd picked him because, out of all the men in the room who didn't yet have a stripper with them, his was the most expensive-looking watch. But now I knew why he was still alone despite the Cartier. You'd think sexiness was an insult the strippers were inflicting on him against his will, rather than, you know, the reason he'd come here.

"You don't want to taste my drink," I repeated, slapping together a fib, "because I have a cold sore."

"I'll take my chances," he said firmly. "Because I don't think that's really vodka in there. And I'm tired of getting ripped off by you women."

Oh, it was too much! Some men, I'd quickly learned, were never happy. The dancers in the club they'd picked were never as good as the ones in the club they hadn't. They whined about it. They wrote *online reviews* about it! The drinks were too watery, the tits too fake, the costumes too cheap, the tits too small, the ATM fees outrageous, the music unlistenable, the bouncers surly, the tits wrong, always wrong, the girls aloof or old or busted. That was their trump word, "busted," and in context it referred primarily to strippers like me who embarrassed them by not laughing at their jokes. Me, I never did see how life could be so bad in a roomful of naked women dancing for you. These guys saw themselves as connoisseurs, but all they were was dreary, the strip club equivalent of someone who goes on a luxury vacation and spends the whole trip needling the resort staff about the substandard amenities.

A real-life deus ex machina saved me from my crabby customer, in the form of the DJ calling my name. Thank God! That meant it was time for my stage set, and I excused myself with no little relief, taking my dishonest drink with me.

Each dancer was called to the stage once an hour to dance for ten minutes. I threw myself at every set with chaotic verve, even when there were only two customers in the room, even when I knew those two customers to be stingy tippers. But most of my coworkers viewed their stage sets as a tiresome distraction from the real business of hustling customers out of their cash face-to-face. Sitting with men was by far the most reliable means of parting them from their money. Up close, they rarely had the balls to stiff us on our tips, and if they did then we could simply walk away. Stage sets were merely live advertising: *All this can be yours if you spend the rest of this hour giving me your cash.* These guys were there for our attention, not our dance moves. They'd perk up when we opened our legs in their faces, but pole tricks and elaborate choreography did not move them, so why bother?

Well, that's not entirely true. Our *female* customers adored pole tricks and withheld their tips from all but the most impressive acrobats, which I patently wasn't, having converted most of my upper body strength into depression in recent months. At first, I was lonely for the companionship of women I didn't work with, and wished I was more skilled on the pole so they would talk to me. Liv, who could comfortably scale the pole for hours, told me my wishes were misguided. These were rarely good strip club citizens. Dancing for them meant dodging their drunken gropings and listening to them complain about how much easier our job was than theirs. This was at the height of the pole fitness fad, and these women wanted to talk shop, despite the fact that we danced on a pole for money and they did it to maximize their core strength. If we met their eagerness with anything less than slavish avowals of sisterhood—meaning, if we pressed them to tip—they pouted. They wrote nasty online reviews, too, the upshot of which was usually that we treated them coolly because we were jealous, ugly, and (say it with me now) busted.

Not all women were like this. Sometimes the sisterhood was real. I vividly remember one slow evening when two Finnish flight attendants came in, both in uniform. It was like the setup to a porno. "This isn't a Chinese restaurant," said one Finn, backing away, but the other grabbed her hand and pulled her into the club. The few customers in the room, all of whom had stopped tipping three songs ago in an act of cheapskate solidarity, peered at them curiously. The first flight attendant ordered two picklebacks, which tickled me. Such an American choice of shooter for these Nordic glamazons.

They weren't particularly forthcoming with the dollar bills—they hadn't expected to need them, in fairness—and anyway, for once, none of us cared. An anarchic mood overtakes a strip club when the cash flow stops. We resented the men in the room, who *had* expected to need cash here, for refusing to tip but also refusing to leave. We had nothing better to do than rain camaraderie down on the flight attendants.

"I have realized, talking to you fabulous women, that our jobs are almost the same," declared one Finn tipsily—the one who'd been initially reluctant to stay. Her gleaming blond hair had begun, tendril by tendril, to liberate itself from the harsh bun in which she'd contained it. "We go to work, and men talk to us like we're stupid. And we have to respond as if we don't realize they think we're stupid."

"*And* they're always wrong," added the other. "About *everything.*"

That got a cheer from all of us, at which point the last few men in the room left—wounded, I think, once they realized we genuinely enjoyed the flight attendants' company. It's a bad idea to let a customer hear what your real laugh sounds like.

We took a photo together. One of the Finns took the picture: her friend at the center of an adoring stripper semicircle. She was even lovelier all flushed and loose like this. She was so pretty she made the rest of us look extra pretty, as opposed to the women whose beauty can only make everybody else seem uglier in comparison. Hers was contagious.

The Finn who'd taken the picture texted it to me. It was the one and only text exchange we'd ever have, though I still think about her, and wonder if she ever thinks about us. "Thank you for spending this time with us," her text said. "I'm sorry we couldn't give you more money."

———

As I lurched tentatively back onto my feet that summer, I didn't feel any better than I had in the last few dire months before dropping out of college. Not that I expected all my problems to be solved by any job, even one where I got to wear fishnets to work every day. But stripping was a particularly tough job to do well in the midst of a months-long, objectless depression that made even showering feel like an impossible task.

I was making as much money at the King's Castle in one good night as I'd made in a month at other jobs, but it had to be one *good* night. Most nights were average, and some were downright awful. Bad nights were a problem because I'd come a long way from the weeping girl with a single dollar in her pocket—I was now hooked on money. The shy romance I'd always had with clothes shopping turned obsessive now that I had thousands of dollars to devote to it. My excursions to the mall had lost all friction. I no longer checked price tags, did no internal math to decide what I'd give up if I bought this dress or those shoes. Then, invariably, after every lavish spend-fest, I'd have three bad nights in a row, and the depression came roaring back, asking me just who in the hell I thought I was, shopping like I was rich or something.

The thing is, a stripper *has* to shop to stay on top of her game. Near the Castle was a sex shop where strippers got a 40 percent discount on lingerie, which allowed me to build an inexpensive wardrobe of work costumes. But what about the makeup, the eyelashes, the mani-pedis, the haircuts, the hair removal, the perfume, the drugs? A customer had once left the club entirely because he'd been so turned off by my gnarled, unpampered feet. My toenails were the only thing wrong with me, but only one thing needed to be wrong here in the temple of feminine perfection. It costs a fortune to maintain beautiful feet when your job is to spend six nights a week dancing on them in high heels, to keep your hair looking sleek and healthy when you have to abuse it with a curling iron every day.

My coworkers must have noticed how much time I spent sniffling in the dressing room. Frankly there was always *some*one sniffling in there, but those women cried briefly and for a reason, while I cried, more typically, at length and at random. But similar rules apply in the strip club dressing room as in a men's locker room: Keep your eyes to yourself, and if anything untoward seems to be happening, it's not your business. The only coworker who ever addressed my behavior was even newer to the job than I was—she must not have known the etiquette yet. Her weird choice of nom de guerre was Ann, an unadorned name that never sounded right when the DJ announced one of her stage sets. (Imagine it now, a deep-voiced man using his best put-your-hands-together voice to say "and now welcome to the stage: ANN!")

"Are you okay? No, I mean," she corrected herself, "you're not okay. I can see that."

Her question asked and answered, I looked up at her with wet eyes, unsure of where this conversation could go.

"Do you want to talk about it?"

"There's nothing to talk about," I mumbled. She nodded, probably assuming I meant things in my life were *so* fucked that I didn't even know where to begin, as opposed to what I did mean, which was that I was just as curious as she was about why I was crying.

We chatted a bit, and she learned that I'd just dropped out of school, while I learned that she was starting her freshman year in the fall. That made her the only stripper in the place who was even younger than I was, which made me emotionally itchy—I'd come to take pride in being the baby of the dressing room. On top of that, Ann was blessed with golden-tan sorority girl prettiness, which I noted with dim jealousy somewhere in the part of my brain that wasn't focused on crying. I was still prone to jealousy of the ways other strippers were attractive that I was not. I hadn't yet slipped into that easygoing, temperate stripper's way of relating to my coworkers and their beauty. Ann, though this was only her second day at the club, had that mode down pat.

She showed me a picture of her boyfriend, a much older man about whom the kindest thing I could think to say was that at least the shadow from his bucket hat hid most of his rodent face.

"Beautiful," I said. It was the wrong word, but she'd caught me off guard with how profoundly hideous he was. Then she asked me whether I wanted to come out with them after work to a place where I could make some real money, and the equation solved itself in my head. One middle-aged scumbag in a bucket hat + one young and outgoing stripper girlfriend + one invitation to the lowest earner in the dressing room to "make some real money" = pimp. I declined the invitation, and she thumbed away my running mascara before leaving the dressing room for her stage set, telling me to let her know if I changed my mind.

The next day, Ann was gone. Edina told me she'd run out on the last hour of her shift with a customer. She'd called the club in the morning to say she was in Detroit and she quit. The biggest surprise was that she'd called.

That same day, maybe picking up on the fact that I'd become prey for the Anns and the Bucket Hat Rodents of the world, Liv urged me to harpoon a whale—to make one of the richer and more generous men into my personal regular customer. "A whale gives you job security," she said. "Otherwise, every day is a struggle. Not to imply that, like, your life is a struggle . . ."

"No, no," I said. "Imply away."

Liv had noticed my reticence with the customers, my general desire to get away from them as quickly as possible. It was biting me in the ass. I was the only dancer in the club who preferred grinding onstage for singles to slowly draining a guy's wallet at his table. The explanation was simple. Onstage, I didn't have to talk to them.

I could blame the customers for my standoffish attitude, and you'd probably believe me, but I must be fair. This was 100 percent free-range zero-antibiotics-added Rax's problem. As a girl, I'd been so shy with men and boys that I could not force myself to speak to any who weren't my father. I eventually developed an erotic interest in men, which helped. Flirting, asking a man about himself, these behaviors came to feel natural—with men I wanted to sleep with. But traces of my girlish fear remained, so that I struggled to chat up any men I didn't find attractive. In a strip club, that ruled out most of the customers. I fished tadpoles over and over again, sexy young men who were too broke for the club, while tips from my coworkers' whales paid my bills. In the delicate strip club ecosystem, I was a parasite. Mine wasn't the only ass getting bitten by my behavior.

Luckily, I harpooned a whale.

It was a complete accident, as are most instances of me being good at my job. My stage set had just ended and I was taking my customary lap around the room, holding out the garter on my leg so that the customers who hadn't come up to the stage to tip me had an opportunity to do so now. (This is admittedly a pretty strained use of the term "had an opportunity." What they really had was me, smiling in their faces, refusing to walk away until I'd parted them from at least one dollar.) As I collected my tips, I noticed an elegant man in his fifties at a table with a young one. The older man was animatedly gesturing with a cocktail stirrer, and I caught a snippet of his lightly accented lecturing as I approached.

". . . which we can clearly trace back to Alcibiades' speech about the cleaving of the original human soul in the *Symposium!*"

"Aristophanes," I said.

Both men blinked, looking a little dazed.

"I'm so sorry," I said, reddening. The younger man turned back to his silver-haired friend, clearly hoping, as many customers did, that I would give up on my tip and go away if he was rude enough. But the older man's eyes hadn't left my face.

"I did mean Aristophanes," he said. From his billfold he withdrew a twenty, so new and crisp that it stuck to the others. He tucked it into my garter. "Very good."

From then on, Dimitri the classics professor came to talk

about Plato with me every week. That was all we did, talk Plato, and as long as I stayed sharp and engaged, the twenties kept flowing. I found the exchange easy, having begun to miss the sharp and engaging Platonic discussions of college. Edina looked at us with suspicion at first—was this yet another of Rax's handsome hobos? But Dimitri was well-off, or at least generous, on top of being fun to talk to. He was the only type of customer I ever stood a chance with: a guy who thought it was cute when I corrected him. He was still condescending to me, but at least this way I could do what I wanted while being condescended to. I could even tell him to go fuck himself, I learned, as long as I giggled and touched his bicep when I said it.

Weirdly enough, those talks with Dimitri helped convince me to take another stab at college. Having him as a customer meant that my income at the Castle was finally reliable, which gave my depression some space to ease up. As the fog lifted, I looked at my former classmates with new anxiety. They were advancing towards a goal that I'd recklessly abandoned; they, and not I, would have degrees in two years. I didn't even know what I'd do with a degree once I had one, but what I *really* couldn't stand was feeling myself get left behind.

I reenrolled, and the Castle had a big party for me on my last night, which also happened to be my birthday. Edina baked a cake for me which read: HAPPY 21ST TO OUR BABY, LOLA! WE WILL MISS YOU! That had been my name at the club—Lola.

I would miss the Castle, and I would especially miss being Lola, who took no shit and made great money. Now that I was leaving, it felt like Lola, and not I, had learned the secrets of maintaining a sexy hairstyle in the humidity. She could walk gracefully in heels, she could set firm boundaries with men, and she'd even been generous enough to pay down that wastrel Rax's considerable credit card debt. Why was I giving up a persona of such power? To go back to sleepy Annapolis and read a thousand long-ass books about what it meant to be alive?

Liv was glad for me that I was going back to school, because it was what I said I wanted, but she had to admit she agreed with me on that last front. "School and books can all wait. These are the years for making your money," she said, helping me stuff the night's cash into my gym bag. Edina nodded fervently, dabbing her eyes—these goodbye parties always brought out her sentimental side.

I'd always been told to be patient, study hard, work hard, be responsible, and eventually the money would come—a reward for making all the right choices, the lollipop after the root canal. Now here was Liv, pointing out that the time for my money was *now.* That there was no need to be patient, that here was something I could grab whenever I wanted and indeed I'd be stupid not to. I saw what she meant: at twenty-one, I still had plenty of time to rebound from the nightly hurt I was putting on my knees as I crawled and bounced on them, shredding their ligaments, bruising them purple. Then, too, I had five or six years left of sweetly telling men I was stripping to pay for college, an evergreen moneymaker of a lie.

"All that, too," Edina agreed, "but come on. You're a baby. No way you can do books and school right now."

I needed to hear that. For one thing, it strengthened my

resolve to go back—I've always had an easier time committing to things that someone else has confidently predicted I can't do. But also, Edina turned out to be right that I was a baby, and it was helpful to remember the way she lovingly excused me for it. I was too immature to take school seriously, and I couldn't look at my immaturity fondly the way she could. Once the school agreed to take me back, I lost my drive to chase my degree and spent my last two years of college in damage control mode, forever catching up on work I had no real interest in. And every time I didn't do my homework because some man wanted to take me to a party that evening, every time I snorted a Percocet instead of going to a lecture, I heard Edina's warm, patronizing voice: *Come on! You're a baby!*

I graduated college two years later by the skin of my teeth, with a C average and no job opportunities in my future. True, that was partly because I'd half-assed my education, but mostly the problem was that I was yet another twenty-two-year-old with a bachelor's degree and nothing else going for her. Right as I was graduating, it was explained to me by the culture that I was really supposed to have a couple internships under my belt by now, ideally in the field where I wanted to start my career. What field was that? I didn't know. I didn't know from fields. Writing, question mark? Or, failing that . . . anything, question mark?

My résumé was useless, even when I proudly presented my brand-new bachelor's degree at the very top of it. Employers with blazer jobs in desk-offices weren't impressed by my history of food service and other customer-facing positions. After months of fruitless job searching, I began to hear the siren call of one particular customer-facing position: legs spread, ass shaking. Money, lots of it, leaking out of my straps and garters.

I didn't want to go back to the Castle. Anyone there who remembered me from my first stint would remember me primarily as a teary-eyed parasite of other dancers' money. I was *not* a baby anymore, dammit. I wanted to try again somewhere new, where I could be smart and calculating from the start, and no one would have to know that I ever hadn't been.

I went to an unfamiliar club to audition with my trusty old gym bag full of wrinkled costumes. I was pleased to realize that both bag and costumes still stank of freshly showered girl and Victoria's Secret body spray, a one-two punch that I'd come to think of as my personal smell. Now that I no longer wore them for hours a day, my Pleasers crackled stiffly against the spread of my sweaty feet, but they'd mold themselves to me again in no time.

The audition went fine—not ten-dollars-for-two-minutes'-work fine, but fine. I wasn't green anymore and therefore I didn't care anymore, which meant my money would be both better and worse. Some men rip you off when they can smell your inexperience, others get off on their generosity with the fresh meat. I'd have to figure out the rhythms of my money from scratch. I would need to harpoon a whole new whale, or else dig up the last one's carcass from the prepaid cell phone where I'd had his number saved.

I danced on the new club's stage as unenthusiastically as my old coworkers had on the Castle's, protecting my knees, saving my energy for one-on-one time with customers. When my song was over, I put my clothes back on and met the club's manager in the dressing room. She was a big harried woman with sleek black hair falling down her back, and she did not seem happy to see me.

"Fine," she said. "Can you start tonight? What do we call you?"

"Lola, please."

"Already got a Lola," she said irritably. Everything she said to me the whole time I worked for her, she said irritably. "Can you be Sasha? We just lost our Sasha."

"Fine," I said.

A new name to remember to answer to; a new name for men to react to in some new way. I supposed I would have to be Russian this time. I began idly dreaming up my new sales pitch: a Russian coed, a vodka drinker. Severe eyeliner and a burgundy-red dye job, why not. *Hi, guys, I'm Sasha. Something something the old country. Spasibo!* I'd miss Lola, sure, but at the end of the day it made no difference what they called me. The power was what mattered—the power, which my supposedly invaluable degree had failed to confer, to earn a living.

Anger Management

On weekdays, I barely had a father. He worked twelve-hour days and then sleepwalked through his evenings, his silent exhaustion filling our home like a gas. Maybe he was saving the last of his energy for bedtime, when he would ask me with great seriousness which of my stuffed animals would be joining me in bed for the night.

"Platypus!" I usually piped up—I've had a stuffed platypus since I was a baby, which was and is awesome.

He'd nod, unsmiling, and we'd shake on it. It amused us to treat these interactions like they were important business deals.

I understood that the time I spent with my dad on weeknights was degraded, somehow, by whatever happened to him during the day. He went to a place called an office in the mornings before I even woke up, and I guessed he was tortured there all day long before returning to me in diminished form for a late dinner. Thanks to his unforgiving schedule, we ate later than any of my friends, which embarrassed me when they came over and were fully starving a good hour before dinner would even be in the oven. On the nights when he read me a bedtime story, he fell asleep before I did.

On weekends, though, he was all mine.

I decided that my father must be two different men, and when it came time to decide which of the two I preferred, there could be no question. Weekday Dad was short-tempered, exhausted; he seemed about ninety years old, crotchety and weary. Then he got into bed on Friday night and woke up the next day as Weekend Dad, whistling, lively, seeming only sixty years old. (In fact, he was in his early fifties.) We marked the transition between dads with his homemade brunch, served to overwhelming effect on Saturdays and Sundays.

Every Saturday, I trotted into the kitchen to observe him in action. My mother wouldn't come within a hundred feet of his meal preparation process, but I loved the greasy-smelling bedlam. Empty eggshells littered the countertop and at least one pan smoked dangerously on the stove at all times, warning my father that it would burst into flame if he wasn't careful. Sometimes his pans did burst into flame, because he was never careful. It terrified me no end but he always laughed it off, slapping a lid over the offending pan. When he removed the lid again, the fire was gone—*ta-da!*—and I felt silly for worrying about something he'd had under control all along.

As a kid, I was a nightmare to feed. I had a rider to rival a rock star's. Cheese was tolerable only on pizza, nowhere else, and that included cream cheese—it may have had little in common with cheddar or Swiss but I consigned it to my personal *No* column as soon as I first heard its name. Anything that smelled too pungent was also out of the question. I ate no mushrooms and nothing green. But at my father's bountiful brunches, which I'd recognized as special, I went out of my way to be more tolerant. I sensed that it was important to him to feed me, and I tried to give him lots of chances to do things that were important to him; life was easier that way.

When I was three years old, my mother and I forgot my father's birthday. Well, really my mother did—I've always been inclined to let myself off the hook, even if he wasn't, seeing as I was *three*. The whole story should be roughly that long, because who cares? He would have been turning fifty that year, which is entirely too old to do what he did that day: throw a tantrum.

"Tantrum" might be too frivolous a word for it. Maybe "hurricane" would be better. Maybe "terrorism."

The whole story of the birthday-forgetting, I heard from my mother later. I don't remember it. I don't remember most of what he did. I only have a single vivid memory from that morning, and it's the earliest memory I have, period: My mother and me cowering in the car, her body shielding mine in a protective hunch, while she dialed the cops and my father pounded at the car window. Even in this memory of my mother's cool heroism, he's the only thing I can see. The garage door was open and the car running, and I was thinking the word *escape, escape, escape* on a scared-shitless loop. But we didn't escape, no. He calmed down after talking to the cops. No one was arrested, no one kicked out of the house.

Years later, the first time the rage was in my chest instead of his, I remember thinking it: *Uh-oh.*

What his fits of temper taught me is that rage is a hot potato.

Force yours into someone else's hands and it'll burn them, not you. I kept sucking all my emotions down myself until I was an adult, assuming I was voiding them like everything else I consumed. I wasn't. I sure looked meek, but inside me those big elemental feelings were beginning to melt. I never expect anyone to take my rage any more personally than they'd take a natural disaster. I roar long and loud and feel like the only person in the world for as long as I'm doing it. But a roar can't go on forever, and when it ends, there I am, not even the only person in the room, much less the world. And now everyone else in the room is afraid of me.

The forgotten-birthday incident certainly wasn't the first time my father lost control—young as I was, I could see something a bit rehearsed in the way he threw his tantrum. But it was the first time he included me in his wrath, little me, toddling around with my platypus in one hand and the fingers of my other hand wet in my mouth. I folded into myself that day and never quite unfolded with him again, not realizing until years later that a folded-in person is angrier than any other kind. I already wrote that he often fell asleep during my bedtime routine before I did; I didn't want to include that I always left him there, snoring in his chair by my bed until he woke up on his own, because I was afraid of what he might do if I disturbed him. I still adored my father, but I worried constantly that I might provoke his anger a second time. I hadn't known it was his birthday. What other dangerous things didn't I know?

My father and I began spending much more quality time together in middle school, maybe because he'd taken a less demanding job, maybe because I didn't have many other friends. Throughout elementary school, there had been birthday parties to which the entire grade had been invited. There had been at least the illusion of inclusivity. In middle school, we learned about something called "cliques," and I realized I wasn't in anybody's, was in fact kind of a loner. But my dad was there to pick up the social slack. And whaddya know, he was pretty good company.

Those last few years before my parents' divorce were a golden age for us. I'd never known my father like this before—he worked so damn much that I'd never had the opportunity to. He did try to play with me in earlier years, but he was often so exhausted that he couldn't follow the rules of a simple game, much less the laws that governed the richly imagined alternate universes where I and my Barbies liked to spend our time. But as a teenager, I got easier for him, and vice versa. It turned out we dug a lot of the same things, and he could be Weekend Dad more often for my benefit.

Our weekly dates were simple. I met him at his office in Georgetown, dressed to kill in my Tripp pants and fingerless fishnet gloves. We went to Clyde's and ordered black & white milkshakes, cream of crab soup, and cheeseburgers with fries— luxe food that left us deliciously woozy, groaning with pleasure. Afterwards, if his good mood held, he would take me to Barnes & Noble to pick out a book. The challenge was to ensure that his good mood held.

It started with the milkshake. He specified that he wanted a black & white milkshake—vanilla ice cream with chocolate syrup—and *not* a chocolate milkshake, and not a mix of chocolate and vanilla ice creams, either. No one ever knew what the

hell he was going on about, and so he always received a chocolate milkshake. And he ordered every dish this way, with some
critically important twist whose execution (or lack thereof) had
a lot of power over him, while I watched uneasily. His moods
were delicate. Anything might bring on a bad one, and not
much could stop it.

It gave me ulcers, how precise he was about food. So much
could go wrong. The way he ordered led to many Abbott and
Costello–like comedies of errors. He was particular about which
kind of cheese could appear on his cheeseburger: American
only—restaurants that didn't serve it were pretentious, hateful places. He insisted that buffalo wings be "double-dipped," a
practice the majority of kitchens had never heard of and that I
still don't understand myself. Bacon was a trauma. No kitchen
could burn it enough. Crab cakes were too small or too bready
or employed a variety of crab that was not local to our area,
which he found ridiculous, considering how good Maryland
blue crab is.

But he never complained about this stuff to his servers. I was
the only one who saw his disappointment, helplessly watching
it annex more and more of his mood until he was mostly disappointment and the outing was ruined.

There were things I could do to tip the scales back. Sometimes joking animatedly would do it—if I caught him with the
right punchline at the right moment, he'd forget everything that
had just gone wrong and laugh his way back to the light. Asking
him for advice brought out the best in him too. He gave great
advice for managing middle school miseries, often getting so
caught up in my preteen melodramas that he forgot to be sad.

If at the end of our meal he didn't have the energy to go to Barnes & Noble, I knew I'd failed.

Mostly, we enjoyed our meals together—he without a second thought, I with thousands. However much fun we had, I couldn't stop scanning the horizon for potential sources of disappointment. Disappointment became self-pity; self-pity could become, had repeatedly become, rage. I would not be caught off guard when the next explosion came.

It doesn't matter how well I remember the moments before and after a particular tantrum. His rages themselves are missing. My inner editor has snipped away and burned the film of those scenes. I couldn't tell you what my beloved father's anger was like if I wanted to. Maybe I don't want to. Maybe I still want you to like him.

When my ex-husband and I began dating, he loved that I had a temper. He explained to me that most women refused to show how they really felt, relying instead on passive-aggressive signals that he hated interpreting. None of that with me. When I felt anger, he knew all about it. It was refreshing, he said.

I loved the idea that my temper was refreshing; I especially loved it in this context where it was better than what other, lesser women were doing. Here was my anger problem, one of the worst things about me, and here was a man telling me it was actually one of the best. Other men just hadn't understood me like he did. I didn't follow the logic as far as I should have, didn't ask myself why this guy might be putting ideas about the inherent flaws of women in my head. I married him instead.

He, for his part, never succumbed to rage, or so it seemed.

In fact he succumbed to rage all the time, but on the surface he was pathologically calm. When I tapped one of the veins of his underground fury—when I went out with my girlfriends, say, or when a meal I'd made for him went wrong—he only grew calmer, icier, haughtier. This added a surreal element to the infrequent acts of physical violence that he inflicted on me.

One day, I confronted him about a woman he'd exchanged phone numbers with at the nightclub where he worked. All night I'd been waiting for him to come home to me, while he was out with her until sunrise doing God knows what. I'd spent hours crafting the most rational case, one that was sure to convince, and now I presented my arguments.

We were sitting on opposite edges of the bed, our usual sparring positions. I was trying to keep my temper at a low simmer. This was how it went with him. I had learned to keep a lid on my heat for a good long time, but now, close to the end of our relationship, he'd adjusted. If I could remain calm for an hour, he would simply pick on me for two.

Hour two was coming to a close now, and I'd come no closer to besting him. He stood; I flinched.

"Keep talking," he said. "I just need to grab something from the other room."

Need to *grab* something? What the fuck? My pan was smoking now. But I'd lost so many arguments by letting it catch fire. I wanted so badly to get it right this time.

He returned holding an airsoft gun, the sort of thing a little boy might fire at a can in the yard. "Sorry about that. Go ahead."

I knew I needed to stay on message no matter what he

threw at me. My eyes on the airsoft gun, I tried to resume my argument.

Casually, he fired a pellet at my bare thigh.

"What the hell?" I asked, more surprised than angry. The pellet had left a pink mark that was already fading.

"Calm down," he said, and fired at me again. Shaken, I tried to keep talking. How absurd, that I tried to keep talking! He fired pellets at me to make me jump and then fired more of them at me for being so jumpy. Didn't I trust him not to hurt me? This, he'd decided, was what we were arguing about now. I forgot what had originally upset me and tried to absorb each pellet as non-reactively as possible. This was a game to him, and because it wasn't a game to me I could never win it. He fired as many pellets at me as it took to set my smoking pan ablaze, and I reared up roaring, full of sobbing fury. Then he leaned back, serene, soothed by my impotent anger.

It's hard for me to avoid reflexively saying how easy I had it with him. After all, airsoft pellets don't really hurt and it's not like he was screaming in my face. I worry that I'm complaining too much even when I just *remember* this stuff; he's that deep in my head to this day. Some part of me never stopped being his accomplice. It's the part that never learned how to stop feeling the rage but figured out, at least, how to direct it inward instead, where it wouldn't be mocked. For his part, he liked that I fought back. He needed my fighting spirit—if I stayed as calm and soft-spoken as he did while he picked me apart, how would he know he'd picked me apart at all?

He seemed to be baiting me for ever-stronger reactions that

he could then label as crazy. If we'd stayed together much longer, he would've goaded me into knocking out his teeth or blacking his eye. I must have been dimly aware that fighting him with everything I had would have glued me to him for life. If I'd ever panicked like a cornered dog rather than an overwhelmed baby, if I'd socked him in the jaw just one time, the shame would have drilled holes through my resolve—I wouldn't have had the guts to leave.

This was the most important lesson I learned as my father's handmaiden. The beginning and middle parts of a rage feel good for broken, self-destructive people like us. Hitting my ex-husband would have felt *wonderful*. I still occasionally regret never doing it, in the same moony way other women regret never sleeping with their high school boyfriends. But even a completely justifiable rage has to end sometime, and what then? We pay for every tantrum in guilt, with interest.

Despite the psychological terror with which my father ruled our house, despite my low-grade fear of him that never fully went away, I don't think of him as an abusive guy. I *can't* think of him as an abusive guy. I may have held any number of grudges against him while he was still alive, but since his death I've canonized him. If I ever dared to reopen all the memories of him being cruel and selfish, the uneasy truces we shared after the behavior he never quite apologized for, I don't think I could bear it. Because he would be dead, but worse: because he would be forever unrepentant.

I don't want anybody who loves me to fear me the way I feared my father. I don't want the life of a lonely volcano, puking magma on myself while the villagers flee. In that vein, there's a note that I really want to be able to end this essay on, something like "and that was my last-ever rage," followed by all those useful lessons I learned from it. No. The rage is still there—less explosive, still corrosive.

I felt it when he was lying in his bed in the ICU for the last time, waiting to die. It had been a rocky few weeks, full of conflicting updates on his health, but by now we all knew the end was near, including him. He was jammed with so many tubes that he could barely talk, and in any event his depleted body couldn't summon the energy, so it surprised me when he piped up.

"You know what I'd absolutely kill for right now?" he wheezed. I looked at him, startled. Mischief was all over his face. Then he had to pause to breathe a few breaths. "A cheeseburger. Fries. A shake. I get nothing to eat these days except hospital *khazerai*."

My mother and I looked at each other, amused and unsure, as his nurse came in to futz with his tubes. "He'd like a burger," my mother said to the nurse. "Would a food run be okay?"

"He can't eat that stuff," the nurse said. "I'm sorry."

She left, and my father gave my mother a reproachful look. "You rat," he whispered.

I cornered the nurse in the hall. "Please," I said. "All he wants is a cheeseburger."

She gave me the look that I gave pushy customers at the dog daycare where I worked: *I'm just doing my job.* "He has diabetes. A blood sugar spike could be fatal right now."

It was bubbling in me, warming, rising; its steam crested up the column of my throat. I thought, in an internal voice that was pleasant and reasonable, *You cunt. I am going to rip your throat out.*

"Whatever happens to him," I said, "is going to be fatal right now."

I knew she was wondering, as I always wondered about pushy customers, how long it would take me to back down on my own; I knew, too, that I wouldn't. My skin felt hot. My brain felt hot. My insides were boiling, melting my outsides. *I mean it,* I thought, my thinking-voice still perfectly pleasant. That was always the last thing to go, before I caught fire. *I am going to tear your arms off. I am going to sink my teeth into your neck again and again until you die.* My body wanted to hurt this poor woman so badly. It was yanking at the reins, thrashing against them, and soon my better self would be forced to drop them.

At length, she sighed. "Just the burger? No fries?"

"Of course," I lied.

At the burger place, I ordered a double American cheese-burger, fries, and a black & white shake, all to my father's exacting specifications. My mother and I delivered the bounty to his tray table, where he tried to receive it with the enthusiasm that such a feast warranted. I pointed out that the restaurant had made the milkshake exactly right for once, and he smiled wanly, puckering his lips so that I could hold the straw up to them.

He wasn't up to eating much, and he couldn't hold anything in his hands—I had to cut the burger into little bites for him, hold up each individual fry for him to weakly gnaw at. Neither of us knew what to do about the tears streaming down my face, so we ignored them. The nurse paused in his doorway and began to say something about the fries and milkshake, but whatever look I gave her made her decide to keep walking.

About a quarter of the way into the meal, he leaned back, pleased and satiated. The rage inside me had cooled and congealed; nothing of it remained but the sludgy chill of my sorrow. That's the only thing that's ever left when the glory of a rage dies down. It's just me, and my hurt, and everything good and healthy that I never learned to do with it.

Ten Items

Your parents may be alive and well right now, in which case let me prepare you for something horrible you've never considered: when they die, *you* have to figure out what to do with all their stuff. Yes, you, sitting there with my book in your lap and food stains of mysterious origin adorning your shirt. Today you're just bopping around all hapless, but tomorrow you might suddenly be responsible for hundreds of tchotchkes that you hardly even noticed when they were on your parents' shelves. You have no use for them and yet you'll find yourself terrified to be without them. A death turns your family unfamiliar, making you hungry for something you know, even if it comes in the form of a cobwebbed Big Mouth Billy Bass.

Why can I see your future so clearly? Because it's my present. I'm typing on my computer and sitting on my bed, two objects I bought because I needed them. But what am I surrounded by? There's no pleasant word for it: *crap*. My dead father's, of course. Crystal toddlers on seesaws, decorative ashtrays, framed photos of people I don't recognize, framed photos of people I recognize and don't like, how can one person own so many fucking decorative ashtrays?, cigarette holders! cigarette cases!, pewter baby cups, wood-carved bears, a bright yellow novelty street sign that says CAUTION! YAK CROSSING!, and vases upon vases upon vases. Not once can I remember seeing a bouquet of flowers in my father's house, and yet that whole time he was apparently packing three funeral homes' worth of vases. There's more—there's so much more, we haven't even left the bedroom yet—but if I keep cataloguing it I'm going to spend the rest of the afternoon breathing into a paper bag, so.

Much of this crap belonged to my bubbe, and I'm sure my dad was no happier to inherit it than I was. But at least he had a house to store it all, while I have only a cramped apartment, every last surface of which has been violently annexed by unusable trinkets. Somewhere in this unholy mélange is my father himself, burned to ten pounds of cinders and stuffed unceremoniously into a plastic sack. In death, he too has become crap.

I live in a museum of haunted objects whose ghost torments me every time I walk through the door. During my last move, I nearly managed to throw out some of my father's belongings, but then I'd imagine him tenderly cradling the offending object. "This is my favorite creepy little ceramic baby," he might say, or "A fourteenth decorative ashtray! What a thoughtful gift!" And into a box the thing would go. At best, I'd passive-aggressively do a bad job of wrapping it in newspaper before packing it, hoping it would have the decency to commit suicide in transit, which many of my own belongings did do, but none of his—protected, I guess, by their specter.

I float in a cursed limbo with my father's stuff, resenting it too much to take care of it but missing him too much to throw it away. Nigh on every object he left me is chipped, cracked, or coated in grimy dust. His belongings refuse to blend into the scenery of my home the way mine do—I routinely succumb to sensory overload when I walk into one of these rooms, because my eyes insist on seeing every little thing he left me while my brain insists on acknowledging each one as garbage. It was only when I began watching the show *Alone* that I got truly acquainted with the reality of a crapless life.

Some people say *The Sopranos* is the greatest show of all time, others argue for *The Wire,* and both parties are wrong, having neglected the History Channel's flagship reality show *Alone.*

On *Alone,* ten forty-two-year-old dads are scattered to different godforsaken spits of wilderness with minimal supplies. The object is to survive off the land for as long as possible, never longer than a couple months. Whoever hangs in there the longest without "tapping out," or calling for an extraction via satellite phone, wins $500,000. Some contestants are women or childless bachelors, but spiritually they're all forty-two-year-old dads. By that I mean they're the stoic, muscular hard-asses your dad thinks he could have been, if only he hadn't gotten himself saddled with a wife and kids who say offensive things like "Just ask for directions at a gas station" or "Are you sure that's a safe place for a campfire?"

Contestants are only allowed to bring ten items into the wild, and only items that appear on a master checklist of approved survivalist gear. You won't see any Delft soap dishes on *Alone.* No crystal decanters here—the most luxurious thing contestants can bring is a single family photograph. Beyond that, it's tarps and pemmican all the way down. It's like *Survivor*, sort of, but without any teams or challenges, unless "not dying of exposure in the woods" counts as a fun challenge.

Now, shrewd readers have probably determined based on everything I've ever said about myself that I'm no outdoorsman. I love a good camping trip, but mostly because I love s'mores and places where emails can't find me. I certainly don't watch this show the way Sean does, critiquing specific aspects of contestants' handmade shelters and fire-building skills. That's a forty-two-year-old dad's method of watching *Alone*. My relationship to the show is that of a woman with a searing dad-shaped wound in her heart that pumps currents of punishing acid through her body with every beat. I'm forced to live in a mausoleum. Six years he's been dead and I'm still too feeble to do anything else. I mean, what if my dad comes back? First thing, he'll light a cigarette, and have no decorative ashtray in which to ash it.

I watch *Alone* because it's easier on my spirit than busting out the industrial-sized black garbage bags would be. I watch these powerful people with their ten belongings apiece as they starve and shiver. The pounds drop from their bodies and their hair falls out or goes white. They eat unseasoned fish for every meal—if they can manage to catch fish. Sometimes they can't, and subsist instead on sea grasses and limpets. There are fried slugs, edible tree barks. Mice roasted on spits, and toenails.

Commercials for the show suggest the danger of living so close to bears and mountain lions in remote, hazardous terrain. *The primeval battleground of the woods,* these teasers tease. *Man versus beast!* But with few exceptions, these sexy megafauna give our heroes a wide berth. Dads who watch the show hoping to see their avatars doing battle with a moose will be disappointed. Instead, contestants feud with rats and weasels. Foxes rob their snare lines and destroy their stores of food. The sweeping drama of life in the wild is reduced, on *Alone*, to a starving man chasing a mouse out of his sleeping bag, sobbing. You really know where you stand in life, trying to start a fire in the Saskatchewan wilderness. You need only what will help you start that fire; everything else, you rightly recognize as noise.

God, I want that for myself so badly. I'm enchanted by *Alone* contestants' crapless existence, as romantic to me as a fairy tale. I watch these poor people as their spirits break, as they weep, voiding some rare parasite from their guts over and over, devoured by mosquitoes, taunted by mice, and I think: *Wow! I guess ten items will get you pretty far, huh!*

At the end of every season, one contestant wins $500,000. One thing about $500,000, it'll buy you a lot of crap.

Sean and I first watched *Alone* on the second day of our honeymoon, when just about everything had gone wrong. We'd intended to spend the first couple days camping—at a campsite with a bathroom, not deep in the Saskatchewan wilderness, so we should've been able to handle it. Unfortunately, that camping trip happened to coincide with my getting over E. coli. (Yes, I had E. coli on my wedding day. Try to keep a lid on your jealousy of my glamorous lifestyle.)

It was a clusterfuck. I spent most of that ill-fated camping trip hauling ass through the woods to the campsite's bathroom, green-faced and cursing those rude bacteria who were still hanging out at the party after all their friends had been chased away with antibiotics. On top of that, we had our elderly dog Shug with us, who had never been camping before. At least, I assume she had never been camping before—she was ten years old when I rescued her, but she's a Pekingese, a regal little dog more closely associated with the imperial courts of China than the rugged outdoors. She loved day hikes, but drew the line at camping. All night in our drafty tent, she shivered and gave us looks of utmost betrayal, which was even more intolerable than the E. coli.

The next morning, we made the unanimous decision to give up on camping and get a hotel room for the night before moving on to the next leg of our trip. We picked a hotel more or less at random and, purely by chance, picked the creepiest hotel in the emptiest town in the Berkshires. The whole time we were there, we saw a total of six people in the hotel and town combined. The vibes were, simply put, *fucked*.

All the last-minute stressors had left us exhausted and somewhat insane, giggling with increasingly delighted hysteria every time something new went wrong, and we decided to lean into the awfulness. We'd had the worst possible camping trip, and now we'd picked the worst possible hotel in the worst possible town. What was the worst possible meal we could have for dinner?

"Mexican," Sean said instantly. "It's a Monday night in the saddest town in the whitest part of the country. The Mexican food will be terrible."

We put in an order at the one Mexican restaurant in town, and it turned out he was right. The restaurant's "salsa" was very obviously just unseasoned Dole tomato puree upended into a cup—we could still see the ridges from the can. At that point, I had been laughing so hard and so long at our unrelenting misfortune that my cheeks were sore. Sean had to leave the room more than once to collect himself.

"Okay, okay," I said, wiping the tears from my cheeks. "We have the worst dinner in front of us. Now, what's the worst show we can watch while we eat it?"

"We don't even get to choose," Sean said, trying to channel surf. "They only get the History Channel."

That night, there was an *Alone* marathon on the hotel TV's one functional channel. It's the perfect show for two people who are having such a terrible day that it's circled back on itself and become hilarious, inducing a state of unusually suggestible madness. Our honeymoon may have been a misfire so far, but at least we weren't Correy, thirty, who had to be medevaced out of the wilderness after tearing his meniscus. Here we were bitching about a few measly ridges, while Keith, forty-five, repeatedly puked up the squirrel he'd barely managed to trap in the first place.

Our favorite type of contestant quickly became the man (*always* a man) who enters the competition in a spirit of inadvisable cockiness. He practically skips from the drop-off point to his campsite, smack-talking the other contestants who can't thrive in the wild like he can, boasting that he's better than everybody else at living with only ten objects to his name. Then he immediately makes some critical mistake that forces him to tap out—usually losing one of his objects.

"Time to put your money where your mouth is, brother,"

Sean crowed at one such contestant, who'd been bragging about his survivalist knowledge and acumen just before misplacing his ferro rod. "Show off all those wilderness skills!"

"I'm sure Mr. Big Tough Survival Man can easily make a fire without a ferro rod," I said, despite the fact that I can barely make a fire even with matches and kerosene.

Unspoken between us that night was the fact that Sean had moved into my home only to find every last corner of it already jammed up with my father's crap. He didn't have that much to add to the mix, but he quickly learned that he wouldn't be permitted to put the belongings he did have anywhere. Everything had its place already. There was no room for interlopers—this apartment belonged to me and my father's ghost. Sean tried to shift a few wood-carved animals out of the way so he could set up his computer, but when he came back into the room, the animals and I had staged a coup, relegating his computer to a tiny corner of the desk. Because my bubbe's furs had claimed the apartment's second closet, he was forced to store his clothes in a filing cabinet whose sharp corners tore holes in all his T-shirts. When he watched the *Alone* contestants as they carried their ten worldly possessions with ease on their backs, did some part of him feel envy? Longing? They accepted these lives of deprived inconvenience for the chance to win $500,000, while he did so for a much less comprehensible reason: me.

What I love about *Alone* is that it asks, with unusual bluntness, what a life *is*. What a human is, what it needs to sustain its existence, how much you can take away from it before it starts eating itself in desperation. Even in these brutal conditions, most contestants decorate their shelters. For every person who leaves the show due to starvation or illness, there are two who leave because they miss their home, where their loved ones and all their belongings live.

I doubt I'll ever be able to toss out my dad's old trinkets. In the years I've been shlepping them from apartment to apartment, I haven't thrown away a single one. I don't want them and yet they're pulsing with life. They're cursed objects, charged by his absence. Memory can be mean-spirited like that, taunting you over your lack of strength, your failing willpower. I don't want my home to vibrate constantly with the knowledge that my father is dead, and yet I can't do what I'd need to do to make it stop.

Sometimes, I look around my living room in its junk shop glory and ask myself: *Which ten things?* Hell, take survival out of the equation—if all my basic needs were guaranteed and I could only keep a handful of my father's toys, which ones would I pick? Thinking this way, I can usually stay rational and calm until roughly item number six, when the reality of such a paring down hits me. I can't throw out the spent and useless grounds of his life.

I've taken to watching *Alone* less for the competition itself than for the contestants' introductory reels, which show their homes and details from their regular lives. Most of these people have been dedicated survivalists for years, and their houses are accordingly spare, the idea being, I guess, that come the apocalypse they'll be ready with only the things that will serve them and protect their families. But these people's minds, particularly as they work through what it means to join the cast of *Alone,* are fascinating.

"I've been a wife, I've been a mom, but I sign up for *Alone* and all that goes out the window—it's all about me," says Melanie, fifty-five, with unmistakable glee. "I now have that time to become whatever it is I wanted to become."

My life couldn't be much more different from hers—for one thing, only one of us dresses up every day in eighteenth-century garb to teach schoolchildren the "period-correct" way to churn butter. And yet I still can't help but nod along as she describes the opportunity that awaits her, because my world isn't mine the way hers will be hers as soon as she steps off the *Alone* transport boat. Whether she picks the ten most helpful items off the master list is beside the point. They'll be items *she* picked, and using them will give her the thrill of living with only her own ideas and choices, no one else to blame, no one to ask for help. Whatever existence she carves out on her assigned spit of land will be, solely and completely, hers.

However much I like some of my dad's belongings, I will never escape the fact that they're *his*. Picking up my own stuff, I might think, *This dress doesn't fit me anymore* or *I wonder where I put the replacement batteries for this.* I'm in an ongoing dialogue with my own belongings, one that changes and matures as I do. But my father's bequests only inspire one thought: *dead dead dead.* Trapped inside that relentless chorus, I can't become whatever it is I want to become. I can become a diluted approximation of him—that's all. Living his life, coddling his crap.

Your Pet Is Dying: An Online Life

I had two childhoods: offline, and online.

Until I was ten, I lived offline in an uninterrupted idyll of verdant grass, crystalline skies, and endlessly enriching Razor scooterings around the neighborhood, all of which were tiresome as shit. I don't doubt that social media is making kids anxious and depressed, and I'm grateful to have had so many years without it, but mostly what I remember is having an awful lot of hours to fill. For all the arguments about which toys will get kids into Harvard and which video games will turn them violent, parents mostly just want their kids to entertain themselves. In practice, we had one less tool for entertaining ourselves before the Internet, and once that tool became available, what did we care if it would be bad for us in the long run? What's a long run? I was *bored*. We all were. You can only scoot around the neighborhood so many times before your mind turns, as young minds inevitably do, to trouble.

We tried to brew some up, my friends and I. One reliable method was to wait until a nearby street was being repaved—in D.C. some nearby street was always being repaved—and then dance barefoot on the fresh asphalt, burning our feet to hooves, coating them with sticky tar that was a bitch to scrub off in the bath later. Still, "a bitch to scrub off," that was something. Another popular game was to chuck pine cones into the yard of a local widow who lived alone, whose wild mass of white hair led us to declare that she was a witch. The pine cones kept us safe from her black magic or something—I don't know. Your guess is as good as mine.

By the time my parents finally gave in and allowed me access to their boxy Windows 98, I was officially ravenous for fun. Ten years old and I'd long ago exhausted my supply of ideas. I knew nothing about computers, but I knew, at least, that they were Fun™ in a way that required little input from me. They came with their own games, and in any event the Internet was full of playmates I hadn't gotten sick of yet, who would surely have ideas of their own.

Sensing trouble ahead, my mother immediately told me I could only have one hour of online time per day, which sounded like plenty when she made the rule—I had a limited attention span and couldn't imagine doing anything for an hour enthusiastically, except maybe reading teen romance novels. But the Internet, I soon found, was better than any teen romance novel, which made it about a thousand times better than my life. An hour was never enough.

So commenced an online childhood, followed by a *very* online adulthood.

As soon as my hour began, there was no time to lose. First, I handled my emails, even the ones that any experienced Internet user could have told me required no handling, like the missives from undead serial killers who would hide under my bed and murder me if I didn't forward their threats to at least twenty people. I never met a chain email I wouldn't mass-forward—for one thing I was deeply superstitious, and for another, maybe one of these days a cute boy would respond when I passed him the Digital Blunt.

Then I loaded up AIM, the messaging service to which every millennial you've ever met has lost between two and eight years of life. AIM was like a swingers' club for middle schoolers. There, I taught myself the savvy use of emoticons to suggest that I had a crush without putting anything damning in writing, the passive-aggressive deployment of Vanessa Carlton lyrics in away messages to signal my romantic availability, and of course the sly and endless dowsing for information: *Are you still dating her? Does she still like you? Would you ever date someone who, or a girl like, or . . . ?* My conversational partners were classmates whom I'd never call up just to talk, but the rules, I'd learned, were different here. All sorts of people could cross all sorts of boundaries to talk online.

Best of all, I had my beloved Neopets, the eponymous virtual stars of the online game Neopets. You couldn't have a dog or cat in the all-virtual Neopia, so I raised a pair of Chias, one of many fanciful options designed by the game's developers. A Chia was a fat little bruiser with goofy bangs, like an eggplant in a wig. I needed to keep my Chias in food and toys, and so I earned Neopoints, the website's signature currency, by playing Flash game after Flash game with the gravity of an overworked father pulling double shifts to feed his family. I played happily for months, until I began to feel the same old itch on my skin—the trouble itch.

The most memorable thing Neopets ever did for me was make me popular. I don't mean popular as in "has many friends," but rather in the sense that, on the game's proprietary Neoboards forums, I finally found people whose social rules I could follow. I was, for a brief and glorious moment, one of the Popular Kids.

I knew what the rules were at school, too—what to wear, what to talk about, which soccer balls to kick rather than flee from when they were inadvertently kicked towards me. But I was incapable of following those rules. I did have some friends, but nearly all of them went to other schools, and good luck convincing your local Popular Kids that you do *too* have friends, they just go to other schools. Most days, I ate lunch alone. Admittedly, I was bringing some serious social handicaps to the table. My mother still picked out my outfits, and I had the habit of quoting Mel Brooks punchlines from 1968 when I wanted to be charming. Between my clothes and my patter, I seemed more like a Borscht Belt club comedian than an eleven-year-old in the year 2002.

But on the Neoboards, the rules were different.

Oh, the *shape* of the rules was the same, particularly the part where the rule makers taunted and ostracized anybody who fell out of line. But even the people who ruled the Neoboards became lonely nerds again when they—fine, we—logged off. We'd learned how to gossip, thwart, undermine, plot, and form factions not from doing it to other people, but from having it done to us. We hoped to colonize this new online wilderness according to the oppressive social logics of the old world, which we as targets understood better than anybody. The difference was that here, we'd be the ones pinning the KICK ME signs to others' backs.

I was wary of the forums at first. The conversations there were dull and, I thought, pointless. On AIM, I deepened connections I already had. Even people who didn't want to be seen with me in school could be persuaded, with a few carefully calibrated messages, to talk to me online. Though we used the occasional abbreviation, we were fundamentally speaking English, so these relationships felt no less real for happening online. But on the Neoboards, people spoke in the inscrutable vernacular of the early Internet. They loved something called anime—*an-eem*? *an-eyem*? I didn't know. They demanded to be told your age, sex, and location. They called their enemies "preps." On AIM, I chatted with people I'd never think to talk to on the phone; on the Neoboards, I now had the dubious opportunity to chat with people I'd never think to talk to, period.

I began leaving tentative replies to other users' posts and worried constantly about being found out. Somehow, another user would know to tell everyone that I was a big old dork in the real world, I was sure of it, and then they would all laugh at me and humiliate me. I'd just watched *Carrie* that year and had become chronically paranoid that a big group of people was—at any moment—about to laugh at me and humiliate me. But my careful sallies were better received than their real-world equivalents had ever been, as were the posts I began making myself, and before long I wasn't the Regina George of the boards, exactly, but certainly the Gretchen Wieners.

I found a Regina to serve in the form of InuYasha442, a Neoboards user named for a manga I knew better than to admit I'd never read. (A big part of my life on the forums was "knowing better than to admit I'd never read that manga.") She exuded ease and confidence online, and spoke the Internet's dialects, with all the ^_^ proto-emojis and l33t-speak that comprised the major online languages of the aughts. I didn't know a word of this language when I first made my Neopets account, but soon enough my immersion in the forums made me fluent, an ex-pat from reality.

I didn't approach her right away. Instead, I began leaving replies on forum posts by users in InuYasha442's orbit. I riffed timidly at first, like any novice speaker of an unfamiliar tongue; then, when my replies got traction, I inched closer to her inner sanctum. It was like the part of *The Godfather* when Luca Brasi cozies up to the Tattaglias, patiently making his way through the family muscle until he's deemed trustworthy enough to hang with the top brass. The top brass go on to ruin my analogy by garroting him to death with piano wire, which I must hastily point out InuYasha442 never did, but my comparison mostly stands.

Otherwise, to kill time while I waited for my traps to catch my prey, I began establishing myself as a presence in forums where my future queen did not rule. On the section of the Neoboards dedicated to roleplaying, other users and I would invent characters and worlds and write interactive stories about them. I'd write a paragraph or two about what my character was doing, the other person wrote their character's response, and so it went, a mash-up of Dungeons & Dragons and improv. My go-to character was Morgaline, a faerie healer who was "not beautiful, but imbued with much charisma and magnetism." One couldn't describe one's character as beautiful without drawing ire and mockery from one's roleplay cohort, who could be tetchier than any writing workshop about characters they suspected of implausible perfection. I had to triangulate Morgaline's implausible perfection in other ways.

When InuYasha442 finally replied to me for the first time, I was in a roleplay with somebody else, weaving our usual collaborative story. The other person's protagonist was a woodland ranger with an arrow injury, and Morgaline was inspecting the wound. Things were getting good, or as good as they could get on the Neoboards, where overzealous automatic moderation disallowed users from posting not just "hell" and "ass," but even words that *contained* "hell" or "ass." Morgaline was bandaging the ranger's leg. The leg, as we all know, is adjacent to the dick. That's the sex zone. It was time to party.

I kept checking for my ranger's reply, but when one came, it was from InuYasha442. "o_0" was all she said.

It wasn't an outright insult. But it wasn't friendly, either. **o_0** was a face that connoted "huh!" or "weird." I knew this move of hers, having covertly watched her pull it on other unfortunate forum users. She was planting a reply, attracting her cronies to make fun of me. I didn't have much time to countermaneuver.

Quickly I replied, "Didn't see you there! *sets out some cheese* ^_^"

Cheese, in her dialect, was a punchline. I didn't know, and would never figure out, why it was funny, but I knew it was her favorite joke. *Come on,* I thought. *Let's be friends.*

"^_____^" she said. A warm smile. I was in.

Unlike an insecure teenager, a Neopet was streamlined and predictable: I do X, the Chia does Y. My Chias knew me not as a middle school goober with bad teeth but as their mommy. It was a role I took no less seriously for its being entirely online. InuYasha442 was supposed to be a side quest, nothing more. I wanted to prove to myself that, stripped of all the real-world signifiers that told my classmates I couldn't dress or throw a ball or get a boy to kiss me, I still had an essentially friendship-worthy personality.

Then she and I exchanged AIM usernames so we could chat in real time, which put the final nail in the coffin of my one-hour Internet-use limit. The new rule was that if InuYasha442 was online, so was I. If she was online for hours, I would be online for hours. I hadn't made a close friend in ages. I was hooked. I was high. (Not literally. Though we both got a kick out of trying to trick the Neoboards moderators into letting us talk about weed, we pledged to each other in a private AIM conversation that neither of us would ever try it. Remembering the solemnity with which I once made that lifelong commitment, all I can say is: ^_____^!)

You don't see a lot of people with thriving social lives who spend all day on Internet forums. InuYasha442's rejection was of a more complete sort than mine. I was mocked and avoided; she was exiled. Her enemies would wait for her to bring some hot-off-the-presses manga to school just so they could tear out the pages in front of her. She wasn't Asian, but they still squinted their eyes at her and made the usual me-so-horny jokes to hurt her feelings—as far as they were concerned, glancing blows were still blows. They curb-stomped her Japanese 101

CD-ROMs. It's hard to know how much to believe an online friend's description of her offline life, but I know that last part, at least, is true because *they filmed themselves doing it*. This was well before the days when every cell phone had a high-quality camera, when filming anything was a real commitment.

She and I weren't sure what this friendship was. In my experience, a best friend was someone you pledged your fealty to, repeatedly. "You're my best friend," you had to say, often, lest the other person have even the slightest chance to grow insecure in your love. Hugs were a given—the more bearish, the better. Best friends drew pictures of themselves together and exchanged heart-shaped pendants of which each friend only had half. It was any girl's privilege and her joy to be incomplete without her bestie.

I talked to InuYasha442 more than any other person, but I wouldn't have felt comfortable exchanging BFF necklaces with her. Both our mothers had warned us to stay away from the Internet's many sirens who they said were, to a man, middle-aged creeps pretending to be kids—the *Dateline* Postulate. I knew this wasn't true of my friend, but that didn't mean she was who she said she was, that she wasn't secretly making fun of me. Nobody knew what this weird new social life was made of yet. Nobody knew whether it could stand up under the weight of real love.

Love was one thing, but there seemed to be no limit to how much hate the Internet could bear. In our AIM conversations, InuYasha442 and I spoke as intimately as we would have in a therapy session. On the forums, though, we wrought nothing but destruction, in its meanest and most insecure idiom. I was done with stupid roleplaying games. They were collaborative, creative, and boring as shit compared to the simple pleasure of treating strangers with mindless cruelty. Everyone feared having her random wrath turned on them, and that meant they feared me, too, knowing as they did that I was her right-hand man.

No one had ever feared me before.

"You two are so n assty," complained one user when we were dog-piling him, and I reported him for obscenity: that *ass* typo. His account was immediately frozen. From then on, InuYasha442 called falsely reporting someone for obscenity "pulling a Rax." Online, I was ruthless. I would have been ruthless in person, too, if anyone had given me the chance to be.

Annoyingly, my Chias were dying.

Neopets can't die, but they can starve endlessly, which any once-dedicated user who's been neglecting their pets can tell you is much worse. Whenever you log in, your pet's icon guilt-trips you from the corner of the page, sobbing from hunger. Click through to his page, and he'll berate you with the fact of his malnourishment. "Your pet is dying!" he tells you, in the website's cheery third-person omniscient voice. It's an easy fix. All you have to do is feed your pet a couple times to shut him up for a while. The problem wasn't that my Chias were dying on this day specifically. The problem was that feeding and primping them, once the highlight of my day, had become a distraction from the real game of talking shit with InuYasha442.

Abandoning my Chias to the Neopian Pound was an option, but I loathed to use it. I could neglect and mistreat my Neopets all day long, but they were still *mine*. I'd created them, I'd built up their stats by playing with them every day, I'd spent months saving enough Neopoints to buy them a pair of rather fetching black-and-flame "fire" costumes that made their chubby bodies look like Guy Fieri's bowling shirts, and even if I rarely bothered with them now, I still clung to my parental rights. In the Pound, all the pets available for adoption were crying. My Chias were, too—they just wouldn't stop crying lately—but at least they were only crying from starvation and not abandonment. And they were kitted-out much better than these other loser pets. Right?

The thought of what I'd nearly done was sobering. I immediately stuffed both Chias with as much virtual food as they could eat and sank back in my mother's desk chair. No longer dying, my babies were now severely bloated. But they were two visibly content little Fieris again.

Later, InuYasha442 and I were chatting about how stupid Neopets was, one of our common riffs and one in which I never felt entirely comfortable. Part of being a cool kid on the Neoboards, it seemed, was an eagerness to bite the hand that was Neopets, to post on the site's own forums about what a useless turd of a game they'd made. A more refined version of this practice now happens on all social media platforms, but back then it was a novelty to spit in our hosts' faces at the very party they'd thrown for us.

I used to have actual Neopets, InuYasha442 said derisively. Her lime-green font and purple text background made her words even more unpleasant. *So embarrassing.*

I had actual Neopets then, albeit badly neglected ones, but it seemed unwise to say so. She continued:

That was like 2 years ago

Like I played the games and everything

I had to get rid of that whole account x_x

Sooooo embarrassing

I decided to test the waters:

Some of the games are pretty fun though . . .

She responded with a link I didn't even need to click. I knew that it led to the badger-badger Flash video, which we sent each other to signify something like "Yeah, right!"

I sent her a placeholder reply, a ^_^ or a ~_^, while I did what I knew I had to do. She would never have befriended me if she'd known the sort of crap I thought was fun and cool. I felt feverish with shame.

I went to the Neopian Pound and clicked the ABANDON button, which took me to yet another screen of my sweet little flame-bedecked Chias weeping. My poor neglected boys. One last chance to do the right thing. They asked me, *Do you really want to abandon us?*

Yes. Abandon.

Are you sure?

Click.

Twenty years later and I still cried like an abandoned Chia while writing that.

Call it the end of my online childhood, the beginning of hardened online adolescence. I had genuinely adored my Neopets.

No, I hadn't been taking good virtual care of them lately—I was too intoxicated by hurting people's feelings for a laughing audience, manipulating my way into a popular girl's confidence, and all the other ugly irresistible games of preteens. Remembering the way InuYasha442 and I used to carry on, I feel queasy to this day. Neopets was a game for children, and I'd abandoned what I loved about it in favor of playing out *Carrie* fantasies on undeserving strangers. Is this how reformed middle school bullies feel all the time? Even in this tiny dose, it's hard to bear.

Parents sometimes talk about the moment their sweet kid becomes a monstrous adolescent. One morning, a seething, hormonal hater joins you at the breakfast table and doesn't leave until adulthood. I'm sure this is painful for a parent, but *being* the seething, hormonal hater is worse. Somewhere deep inside me, I still knew myself. I knew I loved cute virtual animals and hated the ulcerating thrill of gossip, even or maybe especially when I was the one doing the gossiping. The problem was, the self I knew had stopped giving the orders. Someone else was in there, jockeying for control. She hated indiscriminately, and she wanted revenge. Her motto was "And then they'll all be sorry."

These years weren't much fun for either of my parents, but they truly pained my mother, who watched me try to respond to my loneliness by mediating my life through the computer. This was precisely the sort of addictive self-sabotage she'd been hoping, with her one-hour Internet limit, to save me from. She, too, had lived many years of a mediated life before she found recovery. She'd believed she'd discovered a loophole with intoxicants, the way I thought I had with the forums. The cultural conversation around Internet addiction was still in its infancy in the aughts—it's hard to say whether she saw it, specifically, as my problem. What she knew was that this was one monkey she hadn't been prepared to wrestle off my back.

I asked her recently whether she felt the Internet made me less sociable, whether she believed in retrospect that I really had been too obsessed with it, knowing what we now know about how far into the real world its tentacles would reach. Did "too obsessed with the Web" look different in 2003, or did she stand by her original one-hour-per-day rule? I'm more online these days than I ever was then, partly out of career necessity, mostly to fill that same old vacuum. I wanted absolution from her.

"It made you more afraid of people than you would have otherwise been," she said simply.

I'm still glad for my online childhood—despite her concerns about how it changed me, it also gave me a facsimile of the friendships and fun that I simply couldn't find among my flesh-and-bone peers. I wouldn't have been invited to my classmates' parties either way, but at least now I had *some*thing to do on Friday nights, something that included conversation and laughter. The people in the computer liked high fantasy, too, and Flash games, and often anime, which I didn't like, so I even got to practice responding politely when my interlocutor raved about something that didn't interest me. Online, I developed versions of the same social skills I would have learned in person, even if I developed them slant.

Regardless, my mother was right. The Internet gave me friends but it also gave me an excuse to give up on making friends. It was true that online relationships were intense and could be rewarding, but those connections were unstable: easily made, easily lost. A user whose conversation I cherished could have her account banned or, worse, find something better to do than hang out online with me. Either way, I'd never see her again. I don't remember my last conversation with InuYasha442 because there was no *last,* per se; there was just a slow trickling-out to silence, a faint sense of embarrassment on my part, at least, for the way we'd spent our time.

Few of us cleaved to the Internet as our first choice back then. Some users genuinely preferred the low pressure and straightforward rules of online friendship, but most of us yearned for more complete fellowship than this. We were a diasporic people, cast out from our societies and thrown together in a territory no one else wanted. However warm our relationships could be, they were encrusted with resentment: we loved each other because we had found no one else to love.

Back in 2020, I spent a few months selling sexy selfies on Twitter to raise money for Bernie Sanders's presidential campaign, which can most charitably be described as a very 2020 sentence. I suppose the website where I plied my trade is named "X" now, but please know that I'm never, ever going to call it that. My friend Sabrina and I would coordinate these hours-long blitzes during which enterprising ass-viewers could show one or both of us a donation receipt and receive either a nude photo or a dick rating in return. These were exhausting afternoons—I'd rate fifty penises in an hour, and I'll admit now that I rated few of them honestly. Look, corners were cut. I can only see so many dicks at once before they start blurring together into one monstrous, chimeric dick.

During these informal fundraisers, I avoided reading my replies, where online militias of motherless chodes congregated to insult me. It wasn't that their barbs were so painful, but that the behavior reminded me of InuYasha442's coordinated strikes on strangers, which made me cringe. But one reply did catch my eye: some man who followed me, with whom I had several mutual Twitter friends, cheekily asked me how much he should donate in exchange for a follow back.

Who knows why we pay attention to what we pay attention to online? His icon wasn't even a picture of him. I had no reason to believe he was attractive or interesting but, somehow, I knew that he was. Despite the ironic flat affect of his posts, his determined fluency in the new and improved online dialect, I could feel it. Twenty years of chatting with anonymous strangers had given me that sixth sense.

For you, I wrote back, *free of charge.* And I followed him back.

Three years later, we were married.

That's the happily-ever-after version, the time the Internet gaveth that made up for all the times it tooketh away. And it's true that finding Sean, my second husband, was the chief triumph of my online life. I've also found nearly every other serious romantic partner from the last ten years on there, in this or that poorly lit corner of webspace. Editors have hired me based on tweets or essays of mine that went viral. About a third of my wedding guests were friends I'd originally met online. Then again, I met my abusive first husband online, too—it hasn't all been good. The Internet is just another place to find people, and it happens to be an unnervingly flat one, impossible to curate. For everyone you meet and love, you stumble upon a hundred users no one could ever love. I was right in my early realization that all sorts of people could cross all sorts of boundaries to talk online. I just didn't realize that meant that *all* sorts of people *would* cross *every* boundary to talk to me, specifically.

Before I followed Sean back on Twitter, he had spent months asking mutual friends from the real world to introduce us. The pandemic, the upheaval—it didn't pan out. We had to meet in words first, flesh later. But I've always excelled at "words first, flesh later," so why not embrace it? In the few agonizing months when we had to talk without meeting and flirt without touching, I relished the challenge of becoming unforgettable through the two screens that separated us. We learned each other's ways and then, when we finally got to meet in person for a three-hour walk around the park, we learned them again.

I'm not as hot for online connections as I used to be—as I was, in fact, for about two decades, right up until I married Sean. The ever-contracting Internet feels increasingly like an abandoned boomtown. The App Formerly Known As Twitter has become a place where porn bots and questionable supplement purveyors hawk their inescapable wares in all directions. I see fewer and fewer of the people I actually follow in my feed. Even if I still wanted to make friends there, how would I find them?

It's enough to make a girl miss the forums, flawed as they were. But I've found an imitation version in a Facebook group for banjo players, one of many that I joined when I started taking banjo lessons. (For the record: clawhammer, not bluegrass. And if you don't know what that means, congratulations on your thriving sex life.) All the banjo groups are packed with useful tips for players and music recommendations, but only this one also includes a hearty dose of nerdy social dysfunction. There are memes that are inscrutable unless you speak the mother tongue of the in-group, and if you ask anyone to explain the joke, you *will* be dogpiled. Posts are brimming with abbreviations whose elaborations I don't know and am afraid to ask. Famous banjo players, blameless enough I'm sure, are routinely raked over the coals for being poseurs. There's even an InuYasha442, equally intimidating and equally anonymous. When he or one of his cronies shows up in your replies, phew, look out! His profile picture is a stock photo of banjo legend Ralph Stanley. I only know that because I reverse image searched it, unable, as ever, to resist the peculiar star power of the Internet's queen bees, however small their kingdoms.

I could become his right-hand man, if I wanted. After all these years, I know which maneuvers will take me there. But I'm not in this banjo group because I love the Internet so much—I'm there because I love *banjo* so much. I lurk, chuckling at some of the jokes and learning about old-time music festivals that Sean and I might like to attend. I ignore the routine melodramas, like the recurring one between players who favor their index fingernail when they strum versus those who prefer to use a pick. (Again for the record: index fingernail.) I never comment, even when I think of a really funny retort to one of the Ralph Stanley guy's many foes. This online group enriches the music lessons and country jams of my real life, but it will never replace them. After twenty years, I know better than to ask that much of it.

Ms. Girl Power

When I was in high school, I liked to pick up men at the bookstore. Only men, in those days—I was still terrified that a woman, being the same sort of creature as me, could see into the dirty marrow of my soul. Men couldn't, or maybe just didn't, and so with them I was bold and forward. I followed a variant on "first day of prison" logic: I'd identify the most attractive guy in the room, walk right up to him, and ~~punch him in the face~~ ask him what he was doing that weekend.

I only treated the Bethesda Row Barnes & Noble like a brothel because I was lonely for romance and had no idea how to make it come to me, the way girls were supposed to. Boys advanced, girls defended. This I knew. But what choice did I have, when the boys I went to school with weren't inclined to hold up their end of the bargain? How did anyone have the patience for girlhood unless they cheated on the rules?

I'd noticed by then that I was expected to follow a number of rules that were absent from my male friends' lives. My buddy Garrett might wander the halls of our high school before basketball practice in nothing but flimsy mesh shorts, his genitals flailing like they were advertising a deal on used cars, but God forbid I wear a tank top that had shrunk a little in the wash. "Rax! Go change that shirt right this minute!" It was irksome, but I'd never considered protesting it. I'd been born to the gender of modesty and subtlety, two areas in which I happened to be defective. Frustrating, but unfixable.

Today, I prowled the bookstore's aisles striking out with everyone I attempted meaningful eye contact with, even in the OCCULT section where I could usually bag myself a weirdo no problem. (The weirdo might attempt to enlist me into some kind of Aleister Crowley sex ritual, but hey—any port in a storm.) I was getting frustrated and cranky. After all, my mother had told me more times than I could count that men only ever thought about one thing. She'd intended it as a warning, not realizing the extent of my pent-up horniness. If men only ever think about sex, well hell, that makes two of us, pardner—saddle up! This logic had worked okay for me in the past, but its flipside was I couldn't face even the mildest sexual rejections without assuming their subtext was that something was profoundly wrong with me. I figured any man who evaded meaningful eye contact was either gay or disgusted. Whatever lessons I'd absorbed about desire, I'd absorbed them ass-backwards.

Defeated, I posted up on one of the benches in front of the MAGAZINES AND PERIODICALS section, the store's sad-girl repository. Even I, an expert at bookstore cruising, knew that the odds of finding a man here were vanishingly tiny. A woman, maybe, only the women flicking through *Us Weekly* struck me as resoundingly straight, and in any event women were surely too upright and holy to go home with strange girls from the bookstore. I may have been a woman myself—a woman-in-training, anyway—but I thought of myself as a creepy outlier, a hormone in skinny jeans obsessively hunting the man who could satisfy her screaming desires long enough that she could think about something else for a few hours. By now, though, I'd given up on my mission. The hormone was now merely looking for something to read.

It was while I was sitting there feeling sorry for myself that I saw one unexpected title peeking out from the very back of the magazines section. *Bitch,* it was called—I read its name over and over in astonishment, unable to convince myself that a magazine was allowed to be called something like that. This warranted further investigation. I grabbed a copy from the rack and read it on my bench, its cover displayed prominently, so that any passersby would know I was cool and into swearing.

But wait—this magazine was most assuredly not cool, I realized as I paged through it. This stuff was for, ugh, *feminists.*

Like any girl desperate to fit in during the aughts, I'd disavowed feminism. These were the years of *Maxim* magazine, *The Man Show,* anti-Britney backlash, romantic comedies starring Mel Gibson as a misogynist who could read women's thoughts. In the patriarchal culture of the fifties, American men treated their wives like children. They doled out allowances and disciplined lapses in behavior. But in the aughts, thwarted by the victories of women's lib, the men became children in their own right, prodding at women, trying to get a rise out of them. Once the rise was gotten, they basked in the he-man woman-hater's Nuremberg defense: *I was only joking! Lighten up!* A girl who found these troglodytes offensive wore a target on her back.

She wasn't a die-hard feminist or anything, but because she was the female authority figure I knew best, I associated feminism with my mom. I'd recognized her daily existence as pretty thankless: doing chores, maintaining order, all while holding down a job. No thanks! I wanted my dad's life of selfish, scatter-brained luxury, his total confidence that someone else would clean up his mess.

I didn't see the difference in their conditions as informed by gender. My mother was neurotic, and my dad was fun. Who wouldn't rather model herself after the latter? I assumed that someday, I'd get to experience the world as a man with a wife, not as the wife. That was, more or less, what girls were learning back then if they didn't make a point of becoming feminists: one part "girl power!" cheerleading to two parts ignoring the battery acid seeping into their hearts.

But, as I kept reading *Bitch,* I realized this was not a feminism I knew. I'd accepted the cultural message that feminists were joyless, hateful, and out of touch. I hadn't expected them to be capable of producing a document that popped like this, full of color and life. Surely the magazine had any number of articles in it that weren't about sex, but as usual, I had only one thing on my mind and beelined for the horny stuff. There were how-to's about sexual practices I'd never even heard of, comics showing women in bed together. Most of the magazine's ads were from sex toy companies. But this was no simple pornography. *Bitch* did something bolder and more forward than porn had ever done for me: told me I wasn't the problem.

How can I describe the glow of that moment, as I realized how many of my unmanageable frustrations had been imposed

from without by a system that benefited from them? *I wasn't
defective*. What a revelation! When my classmates laughed at
me for sleeping around so much, when teachers sent me to the
locker room to put my smelly gym shirt over my offensive cleav-
age, they weren't punishing me appropriately for something I'd
done wrong. They were cattle-prodding me into submission. I'd
always known I was a girl, but reading *Bitch* for the first time, I
began to feel like maybe that wasn't such bad luck after all.

I bought that magazine and strutted it through the halls the
next day like a pet I was taking for a walk, reading it with the
cover flagrantly visible every chance I got. If I couldn't read it,
then it had to be sticking out of my backpack, or perched on
the corner of my desk. Disappointingly, few people noticed,
and the ones who did notice looked away in a hurry when they
saw what I was reading. But I was patient and got what I was
angling for in the form of a sweet older lady named Marjorie
who worked in the front office.

"I'm not sure it's appropriate for you to read that here, hon,"
she said.

Gotcha, I thought. She was a perfect first sparring partner,
too—in her sensible heels, with her freshly set gray hair, she just
looked like an opponent of the cause.

"It's a feminist magazine," I said. "What about feminism is
inappropriate?"

"I'm sure you know what I mean."

"I don't," I said, standing from my bench. A couple other students glanced over curiously. "What do you mean?"

Marjorie looked trapped for a moment and then walked
away, shaking her head. I'd walloped her with a primitive model

of what would become my signature cudgel: *If you make me do a task that doesn't interest me, you are an enemy of feminism.* Once challenged, it seemed she was a meek sort of person under her institutional authority. That was the sort of person I was too, actually, but *Bitch* had given me superpowers. I'd never in my life been more certain that I was in the right. (*Was* I in the right? It depends, I suppose, on your tolerance for high school students seeing the word "bitch" written in 128-point font.)

At first, my "feminism" mostly comprised petty victories like this over—oops!—other women. I wasn't interested in digging in, learning, checking out books on feminist theory from the library. I would attend no meetings and serve on no committees of any kind. That all sounded like mom stuff to me. What I wanted was to live in the euphoria of my feminist awakening forever, the rage and drama of it, without asking any questions that might puncture my feeling of triumph. It was enough for me to have uncovered the secret value in being a girl.

Because that epiphany had been simple, I assumed feminism was, too: every woman who behaved roughly the way I did was in, and women whose behaviors stank of the patriarchy were out. I was used to making catty, cosmetic judgments about other women—all I had to do was adjust the framework I used to make them. The women of *Sex and the City* had always inspired me with their drinking and fucking, and now I could decide, retroactively, that they deserved my admiration because they were properly liberated. My mother, who was always asking me to do some shit I didn't want to do, was another story.

"I've asked you twice now to do your laundry," she said to me once, pleadingly, anti-feministly. *"Please* stay on top of it."

"Why? Would you ask your brother to do his laundry? Or my father?"

She pointed out that it was immaterial to her *who* did her brother's laundry, as he lived in Virginia, where his housekeeping or lack thereof could have no effect on her. As for my father, now that the two of them were divorced, he was, in fact, doing his own laundry.

"He's doing his own laundry *now*," I said triumphantly, "because he doesn't have a *woman* to do it for him anymore."

"Indeed he doesn't," she said curtly, pushing the laundry basket into my arms. "And maybe that attitude on his part is why we got divorced."

Obviously, I did want a woman doing my laundry for me—her. My feminist revelation had mutated in my self-righteous teenage brain, becoming a crackerjack way to avoid responsibility. All I had to do was point out that some chore or instruction had its roots in the patriarchy, which rendered it ethically moot. I still expected that, come adulthood, I would have a helpmeet of my own. I would sit at my desk, hair wild, eyes manic, turning out masterpiece after masterpiece of feminist invective. And in the background, the chores would be getting done—not necessarily by a woman, but certainly by some kind of wife.

"I don't know how to teach you to do it," said my friend Garrett of the skimpy basketball shorts, a little embarrassed, when I informed him that he was infantilizing me by always rolling my joints for me. "Like, I don't know how to explain it."

"It's important to me, not having to rely on men for everything," I said patiently.

"I know you're, like, Mrs. Girl Power now, and I respect that, but I legit do not know how to describe what I'm doing right now. Maybe you could just watch me?"

"That's *Ms.* Girl Power," I said. "No, I mean, it's not 'girl power' at all. I mean . . . Just shut up, Garrett."

Before the Feminist Awakening (B.F.A.), I considered men's behavior only in the context of whether I liked it or not, and I'd always liked it fine when Garrett performed this mildly chivalric task for me. All my relationships with men included dozens of data points like that—favors done or not done, doors held, haircuts complimented, orgasms achieved or bypassed—and none of them had ever seemed particularly meaningful on their own. But After the Feminist Awakening (A.F.A.), overzealous with the force of my emerging consciousness, I changed my mind. I took the idea that "the personal is political" and ran with it as far as it would take me, so that I now believed, in a paranoiac spirit, that every personal thing was equally political. And because my life was so full of boys and men, I had plenty of opportunities to litigate my personal politics. In fact, A.F.A., I was more obsessed with men than ever before.

I'd been what you might call "boy-crazy" since elementary school, when my budding obsessiveness dovetailed beautifully with my peers' dedication to boy bands and the floppy-haired crooners who led them. Those were the days, man—a boy-crazy girl could blend right in, her single-minded devotion to love-feelings looking like nothing more than a temporary, culturally transmitted illness. If my parents even noticed the grease spots on my posters from where I used them to practice frenching, I'm sure they assumed this behavior would pass quickly enough. Maybe it did with other little girls, but as I grew up, I remained perpetually in the pit of some unrequited crush or other. I couldn't climb out, ever.

It didn't help that, as a teenager, I mostly chased adult men—young ones, they'd only just stopped being teenagers themselves, but still. Even if it wasn't illegal, there'd be something morally unbecoming about a college graduate taking a high school junior on a date. These men's adulthood was glamorous and enticing to me: they could buy beer, they had bedrooms into which no parents would walk at the least opportune moment. But adulthood, in a man who's banging a teenager, doesn't translate into maturity. Usually the opposite.

I got used to being treated shabbily by the men I slept with, and so it was a shock to my system, reading in my beloved *Bitch*, that these men actually *benefited* from their cavalier behavior towards me. Of women in general, sure, but I was sixteen, and that meant I was the important one. I could tolerate getting fucked badly, and I'd get over it if the guy responsible never called me again afterwards. When a different man did the same thing a few weeks later, fine, whatever—you've got to kiss a lot of frogs, and so forth. But I hated the idea that these men were dumbly following the patriarchy's recipe, nothing more. I could have been any girl at all. Once again, I was learning that I wasn't the problem. Only, in this case, that made the problem impossible to bear. If men were going to mistreat me, I wanted it to be a special mistreatment just for me, not the same off-the-rack cruelty they peddled to every woman they could find.

———

A few weeks before I left my first husband, Corinne was paying me $150 a night to work the door at a venue called Hank's. She hadn't hired me because she needed another door girl so badly, but because she'd heard from our mutual friends that I needed cash to escape an abuser. She knew, too, that I'd tried to leave him before, and that I kept getting stuck, broke and hypnotized, in the dark magnetism of our life together. Now I was working for her and crashing at her place most nights, hoping the arrangement would give me both the distance and the cash to break the spell. Hiring me was a mitzvah. She was going to bust me out.

"She pays you that much to sit in a chair making change for a few hours?" my husband said during one of our nightly phone calls. "*And* you're staying with her?"

"Yeah, I don't know," I said. "I guess she really needed the help. And it's way easier to crash with her than to get rides back to Annapolis every night."

"Sounds like you've got a little girlfriend."

We laughed off his remark, but it certainly felt like I had a little girlfriend. How else to describe this strange relationship with a benefactor who was also, unbeknownst to my husband, a lover? Then again, if either of us two was to be described as a "little girlfriend," it would have been me. Our relationship only had room for one star, and it had to be Corinne. She had that extrovert's gift of turning every show and party into just another outpost of Corinneland, a realm of which she was the queen and I was the little girlfriend. My liege lady's arm slung low around my shoulders, her royal lips in my hair. I'd never been in love with a woman before—I worried too much about saying the wrong thing, like I never did with men. I respected women more, or at least I put them on the same pedestal that smitten men put me on, which felt like respecting them. I'd put Corinne on a pedestal, too; she just happened to be the sort of woman who was born to sit on a pedestal, looking down at someone who adored her.

Corinne despised my husband because I despised him, but however despicable he was, even she hesitated to steal a wife from a husband outright. She could have—I was unstable, and eminently stealable. Instead, she held my head in her lap after work and daydreamed out loud in her husky voice about what our relationship would be like after I left him.

"I'm going to buy you so many incredible meals after you leave him," she said. "I'll get you an apartment in my building. With a dog. The most useless lapdog in the world, and he'll have nothing to do in this world but love you."

Most nights, I drifted off to the sound of these lullabies. I dreamed regularly of an opulent supermarket, its aisles full of every wonderful treat she said she'd buy me.

Corinne always needed someone to take care of—she hired people to work for her based less on their skill set than their degree of personal tragedy. She didn't care that I was the most pathetic door girl Hank's ever had, constitutionally incapable of handing people the correct amount of change. I kept letting underage people in by accident, too, because I felt like actually reading the dates on people's IDs always took me too long. If anything, *I* was the most useless lapdog in the world, and I must have been a cute one to boot, because Corinne kept petting and petting me anyway.

For my part, I was so relieved to be in love with a woman. This was to be my ticket out—from my disaster of a marriage, true, but also from the bind of romance with men, a knot whose ends never stopped turning in on each other. My love for men had come to feel like a sneaky form of self-harm. When Corinne held me at night, murmuring promises, I felt hot and drunk on the future my husband didn't know I was building, a future that was all the sweeter because it only had room for women. Soon, I would leave him, and his ownership over me would transfer, I assumed, to Corinne. If she occasionally seemed bossy or possessive, that was fine—I'd spent enough time in a different bossy, possessive lover's service to know my place. I brushed her hair, rubbed her back, and gave her head until my neck was in knots.

After a few weeks of this, I got the email I'd been waiting for from my college. A dorm room had finally opened up on campus. I could move in after spring break. The cash I'd saved working for Corinne would cover my deposit towards room and board.

The day I got that email, I went to my shift at Hank's and told Corinne the good news. She crushed me into a hug whose sheer force left me dizzy.

"Oh, honey, I'm so excited for you!" she said. "You're finally going to be free!"

It surprised me, that she used the word "free." Whenever we'd talked in the past about what would happen when I left my husband, the word she always used was "mine."

The whole night, I was walking on clouds. That's a cliché, but what do I care when it was precisely how I felt trying to move through the world in some normal-looking way when my imminent rescue was achieving liftoff in my spirit. I was getting out! None of the customers at Hank's knew it when they pointed out, for example, that they'd given me a twenty rather than a ten, but still I was sure that it must have shown on my face somehow: I was *getting out*! Evacuating hetero hell, at long last, to become a kept woman for my girlfriend-boss.

But, without the ballast of my abusive husband, Corinne and I didn't last a month. Having a hateful misogynist to plot against had been a helpful shorthand for an intimacy that we'd never actually built. It had given us purpose and momentum. What had we ever done together, other than eat meals she paid for while planning my triumphant escape? What did we know about each other? Neither of us dumped the other—nothing that blunt ever passed between us. She canceled plans, I canceled the rescheduled ones, and we faded out of each other's lives. She found a boyfriend and then I did. We had missed our window. All that's left is two women liking each other's Instagram posts, genuinely happy for each other.

I intended to write an essay about my earliest experiences with feminism, and it feels bitterly fitting that it wanted to be about men, too. So often, when I try to think about my fellow women—what we want from our lives, the things that unite us—I end up just resenting men. It's less taxing, intellectually and emotionally. My future as a woman is this intimidating, unknowable wilderness, but the past is easy: so much of my teenage life was done to me by men. They're the ones I prioritized, every chance I got. I may be a feminist, but there's no denying that I've always been an awfully boy-crazy one.

Do I resent men for the very real power they've exerted on women over the centuries, or is it because I've given so much of my own self to the work of chasing and impressing them? By now, I'm mostly an amalgam of old boyfriends' tastes, even down to my favorite restaurants. I love sushi, the Catskills, and the Jesus and Mary Chain—all because some man introduced me to them. I've become Frankenstein's monster, lashing out at my creator. Who might I have become, had I pursued a life's work other than boyfriends?

My youthful "feminism" was lazy and full of holes. I did not, for example, devote much thought to the police violence plaguing Black men and not myself, or to the men in faraway countries who did grueling labor twenty hours a day so that I could have a cheap cell phone and sneakers. I didn't think about women who suffered those forms of violence either, for that matter, or about any woman who wasn't essentially like myself. "Solidarity" was not a word I knew. My feminism, in those days, was all about petty revenge, settling scores. The patriarchal male had stolen something *from me,* and I wanted it back.

Some part of me knew that if I educated myself beyond my golden revelation, I would learn that I had work to do—that the patriarchal male did owe me, yes, but that I owed others, had wronged others. I didn't want to do any work, whether on myself or on the world. I was having too good a time terrorizing my mother over the laundry. Now that I've actually done some of that work, from escorting patients past screaming protesters into abortion clinics to preparing food at shelters for victims of domestic violence, I completely understand why I avoided it for so long. It's daunting, only being able to take such tiny bites out of sexist injustice. Caring for women is harder than raging at men. Though the latter is what really does nothing, the former is what feels, in the moment, like doing nothing.

Even now that I've dated women, I'm still fundamentally boy-crazy. Indulging in persistent, consuming resentment towards men is just one more way to be boy-crazy, one that feels slightly more dignified once you're no longer a teenager suffering from teenage feelings. Still, if I didn't have to take care of myself and earn a living and all that nonsense, I could happily spend every waking hour nursing a crush. I wish plotting over men was a career path—I'd be on the cover of *Forbes* by now. But mooning over one's sexual entanglements is widely considered to be a waste of time, so I had to become a writer and pretend my mooning was in service to the world of ideas. Maybe I originally became a feminist for a similar reason: to lend a bit of dignity to my brawling with men.

Cough-Cough

Click click click except I can't work the Bic so it's really *clk,* all stunted. This is exactly the sort of thing I'm terrified of goofing up in front of my friends. Now here I am, goofing it up.

I've watched my father light thousands of cigarettes. Hundreds of thousands. Lighting them looks like the easiest part, considering what follows: a tattered breath, a full-body hacking cough. Pain, smelly and bleak. But the lighting, that takes one second and you don't even think about it after. Well, maybe *you* don't. Me, I will be thinking about myself not lighting this cigarette for a long time.

Someone offers to remove the Bic's childproof strip for me. That offer is a warning: I'm taking too long. I'm making everybody fidget for want of the experience I can't facilitate.

The cigarette I stole from my parents' stash gets lit eventually. Not by me. I get the first puff, though, a tactful acknowledgment of my sacrifice. The first puff, my Purple Heart.

Some hours later, at home: "Stop *watching* me, dammit." He pauses. That inimitable cough. "Why is it every time I even pick up a lighter today, there you are, staring?"

"So quit smoking," I say. Not much heart in it—embarrassed to have gotten caught studying my father's Bic technique. But more than that, it's just this play of ours has run for too many seasons. Neither of us says our lines with much gumption anymore.

And indeed he is silent. Like he didn't hear me, but really: like he can't make himself say yet again how he's just about to quit, as soon as . . . whatever. As soon as something else happens, some other time. I'm sixteen years old so let's say he's been swearing to quit as-soon-as for ten years. Plus however many times he's said it to everyone else who's ever begged it of him.

None of that matters right now, though. I've seen what I needed to see. More pressure in the flicking finger than I thought—that's all.

Cigarettes, I don't like. That doesn't stop me from smoking them. By the time I'm old enough for them my father has been buying apocalyptic quantities for years. The unit in our house is not the cigarette or even the pack but the carton. Of course I smoke them. They're too everywhere not to.

Before I tried them, I feared taking one drag and finding myself immediately enslaved to Marlboro or Camel. Enslaved like my parents are. It didn't happen, maybe because I know, intimately, how unpleasant it is to serve that master. Hearing my father's gnarly hacking in my head with every puff is something of a turnoff, it turns out.

They disappoint me, usually—all the ways I'm not like him. But being unable to love cigarettes is an unqualified relief. The devil possessing my father has passed right over me.

Weed is different, I convince myself. I'm pleased to fall in with the stoners—they're a low-pressure bunch. We recognize each other's worries and meet regularly to calm those worries with our ritual of shared anesthesia.

I cultivate stonerdom like a hobby. It looks an awful lot like a hobby—all those toys and lingo and new friends. People think of stoners as passive, but as a hobby weed-smoking is actually pretty active. It asks a lot of you. It especially asks a lot during my high school years, when weed is still, with rare medical exceptions, illegal. Buying it, selling it, and having it all require different strategies. You need to know a dealer, invariably an adult man in a bathrobe who uses a rainbow serape as curtains and collects obscure reptiles. You need to know how to roll a joint or pack a bowl; you need, to that end, papers or a pipe. Lighters, matches, eye drops, Grunge Off to keep your gear clean and odor-free. Cash, and cunning. Weed keeps you chill, but it also keeps you busy. I love the busywork aspect of it, how the subsequent relaxation feels like a reward for a job well done. I don't tie this to my father's smoking, to his own desire, obvious in retrospect, for the satisfaction of a job well done.

Suddenly smoking isn't in all the places it used to be, or so it seems to me when I'm little. Restaurants that used to ask nothing now ask, smoking or nonsmoking? (Smoking, always, which sucks. Nine times out of ten, that's the section without any kids in it, other than me.) In a few more years they'll ask nothing again, this time because there will be nowhere you can smoke instead of everywhere.

This habit of my parents' always seemed normal to me. But

things in the outside world change, slowly, slowly, until one day I blink and they *are* changed. People give my father the dirtiest looks inside his smoke cloud now. They hold their noses, they cough goody-goody coughs at us, *ahem, ahem*—nothing like his coughs, the drama of which feels totally earned. In school I learn that smoking is BAD FOR YOU and FILTHY and SMELLY and that anyone who does it will DIE IN PAIN. Out of school I shudder at how much money my father is now spending for the privilege of DYING IN PAIN.

He pretends for as long as he can that he can't see the sun going down. Buying cigarettes used to take five minutes: walk to store, walk home. Now it takes nearly two hours. He drives to Virginia. Says *Gimme every carton of Marlboro Lights you have and will you help me pack up the car, please, I'm sick.* Cough-cough, partly for effect, mostly because that's just how his body ends a sentence these days. He pours the money he saves buying Virginia tobacco into his gas tank, feels like he's getting away with something.

Sometimes I'm in the car with him during these trips and I see the cashiers' faces as he makes his halting, wheezing approach. There are eye rolls. Breaks taken prematurely and with haste. Once, an *Oh boy* mouthed so distinctly I wonder if I'm meant to see it. And, if I am, what I'm meant to do with it—with the embarrassment of my father's need.

He's my hero. Problem is by the end of the '90s I know him to be a filthy, smelly, *weak* hero. Graceless, too, the sorest of sore losers. Smoking is, frankly, all he's got left—smoking and shame about being unable to quit smoking. And his shame's a cancerous thing, quick to kill.

I find myself in its path when I get in trouble with a teacher one day. My crime? Smelling of cigarette smoke. It's not my smoke, I tell my teacher desperately as she writes me up. That only leads her to include in her report that I'm a liar, too.

"I wasn't even in your car for *ten minutes*," I wail at my father when he comes home that night. "Now everyone at school thinks I *smoke!*"

My father doesn't know how to react to my feeling ashamed of him. Ten years of raising me and it's never come up. His own shame metastasizes, claims me as a new host. Not only can he not force himself to quit smoking, he can't even rely on me to tell him it's okay.

He hurls an ashtray at the wall and unleashes a primal, wordless bellow whose vibrations I can feel in my ribs. Then he storms off, his thunderous footsteps rattling the picture frames on the walls and the shards of ashtray on the floor. My little heart is rattling too.

He's smoked cigarettes since he was thirteen years old, but he also used to smoke weed, crack, and PCP. He drank, too, and took pills. Just about the only thing he didn't do was shoot up heroin, the middle-class white person's line in the sand—"The only music I don't like is country and rap," but for drugs.

Piece by agonizing piece, he gave it all up. He defeated cocaine, and life was briefly peaceful, until alcoholism roared to life in him like an uprising and he had to crush it. And weed supported him in these battles—until it turned traitor on him, sang in its mellow voice the same haunting songs that various liquors and powders had sung him his whole life. He had to break that alliance, too.

What I'm sure he wants to say to me—what comes out as a shattered ashtray and, some hours later, an uneasy apology—is that he *can't* give up cigarettes after all that. Not until he's rebuilt everything in him that he needs to rebuild. This work will take decades. He needs his oldest, trustiest ally at his side.

His voicemail greeting, 2017:

> *Hello, you've reached [ten-second interlude of high-octane coughing]. I can't come to the phone right now. Please leave me a message and I'll call you back. [Several more seconds of coughing, during which he can't figure out which button to press to end the recording.]*

Sometimes things seem to be looking up. "I got myself an e-cigarette," he tells me, shyly pleased with himself.

"That's great!" I say. "Those are supposed to be the best for quitting."

"I'm even down to two packs a day," he says. Anytime he wants to give me hope, he claims he's down to two packs a day.

And yet when we speak on the phone the next day, there's that scabrous drag, the purposeful chuffing of smoke from mouth and nose. The two sounds I'll never hear again without looking around instinctively for my father.

"No e-cig today?" I ask.

"Lost it," he says.

Will you please pick up the pace. I'd never say it to him but I sure do think it, often. Tapping my foot, rolling my eyes. Waiting for him to give all that hacking a fucking rest, to unpeel his shoulders from their hunch and force the blood flow back to his face. Cough-cough, cough-cough, cough-cough. *Come on, walk, keep up with me.* It takes us ten minutes to walk a block. Every cough an opus. *His decrepitude is his own fault,* I think savagely, *and I'll be damned if I'll baby him for it.*

Such a goddamn waste of time—trying to bully him into staying alive.

"I wish you'd change that voicemail greeting," I tell him one day. "I hear it and all I can think is *cancer, emphysema.*"

"Bummer," he says, as if I've just told him that tickets are sold out to the movie we wanted to see, not that I'm afraid he is going to die.

And now I feel it myself with every drag of a joint. *Weed isn't as bad for you as cigarettes,* I scold as the smoke singes my throat and tells me in no uncertain terms that it's hurting me. Whether I'm scolding myself or him is unclear. His cough-cough sprays out of my mouth, a sickly wet *I told you so.* It's always been the sound of him giving up. Now it's the sound of me giving up.

My new pet worry is that my clothes smell like weed. I sniff them and turn up no evidence, but maybe that means I smoke too much to even smell it anymore. So I ask others to sniff me. *No, Rax, you don't smell like weed.* But that's exactly what they'd say if they were lying to protect my feelings! The worry replicates and mutates: not only do my clothes stink, but no one will tell me the truth about it. In twenty years, I fancy, I'll have to write the essay about how all my clothes really did smell like weed, because I will have quit smoking . . . in twenty years. As soon as something else happens, some other time.

I exit a particularly rowdy mosh pit one night and see that I have a voicemail from my father's new part-time caregiver, Leslie. I've only met her once, at my dad's seventy-fifth birthday party, where he posted up in the corner of a Spanish restaurant with his oxygen tank and one by one his many loved ones all approached to kiss the ring and eat mediocre tapas. He, for his part, detests tapas, but this was the only neighborhood restaurant big enough to host all his friends. Leslie cried that day. Said, *Your father really is just like the Godfather,* and *he loves you so much,* or maybe it was *I love him so much*—things like that. She's sweet, Leslie. A gentle soul. And there's no one I want to get a late-night voicemail from less.

I walk two windy blocks away from the venue without my coat. I don't want any of these tipsy punks watching me absorb whatever's in Leslie's message. In it, she sounds a little drunk and a lot heartbroken. She calls me "honey." Says my father fell and broke his "tush" and is in such-and-such hospital and would I please call her right back. Here is her number. Here is the hospital's.

I call my father's home number, then his cell. Twice each,

then thrice. I am casting a stubborn spell: If I call him, not Leslie and not the doctors, then he will answer. And if he answers, then this situation isn't what I sort of know it is.

The next day, I tell my boss that I have to go home for a few days because my father broke his tush. It feels important to preserve Leslie's prim, odd phrasing.

I call Leslie from the train, finally. She's still in my father's hospital room with him. I don't think to say thank you. At no point from now until the end will I think to say, *Thank you, Leslie, for everything you've done.* Too many other thoughts to think, I guess, and not enough grace helping me think them. The grief that I know is coming for me makes me rude.

He's sleeping when I arrive. So I talk to doctors, nurses—his "team." No two tell me the same thing. His prognosis is hopeful, no it's not. Back and forth they go. The broken bones are straightforward enough. They can be repaired, his body rehabbed, except for the condition his lungs are in. The hospital can't safely anesthetize him. Any therapeutic exercise that might help strengthen his body he can't breathe well enough to do.

On the wall of his room are written his age, weight, and so on. I read the weight, read it again. Confirm that it's in pounds, not kilograms. No way that number is right, when he's the biggest man there ever was.

I ask the team whether they can at least tell me what the hell happened to land him in here. They exchange looks among themselves and say no, they can't, and even if they could they wouldn't—he tells it better.

"So there's this wasp in my kitchen," he whispers. He can't speak above a wheezy whisper, but his expression is bright.

I nod at him to go on. I should speak, *I must speak,* only if I speak I'll cry, so.

A wasp, a great big stinging mutherfucker of a wasp, milling about right there on the countertop while he's reading his morning paper. *Sauntering,* you might say. *Not in my house, you bastard,* and so he rolls up the newspaper to give the wasp what-for—but as he whacks, he slips. Shatters a leg and a hip [does not say "tush"]. So there he is, splayed out on the floor, nowhere near his phone, totally alone.

He's telling it like a bedtime story. My eyes are little-girl wide.

He doesn't know how long he lies there. Half an hour, maybe longer, the whole while assuming he'd be lying there alone for the rest of his soon-to-be-concluded life. Just when he's writing his last 9th-step letter in his head . . .

"No the fuck you weren't," I say, amused. "You were imagining your obituary, and everyone's eulogies. Beautiful women, weeping."

He acknowledges with a smirk that this may have been the case. Fine, well, just when he's *wrapping things up* in his head, hark—a knock at the door! Two women on some kind of door-to-door sales call.

"And it's in this moment that I get to say something I've wanted to say longer than I can remember," he whispers. Gathers what remains of his strength. Fixes up his face for the punch-line. "Help! I've fallen and I can't get up!"

There's hysteria in how I laugh at this. It's the funniest thing

I've ever heard, less because it's actually that funny than because it's a joke *he's* telling to keep *my* spirits up.

Miracle of miracles, the saleswomen hear him, and are you ready for a double miracle: one of them is an ex-paramedic! She knows just what position to hoist him into, knows to tuck his wallet and phone into the pocket of his bathrobe. There's no way she really asks if that's an exposed bone or is he just happy to see her, but I love him for telling me she does.

The women wait with him for his ambulance and wish him the best once it arrives—but he has one question for them before they part ways. Strange question, bear with him. Is there, by any chance, a dead wasp near the place where he fell?

Mystified, the ex-paramedic checks. Takes her goddamn time about it, too. The current-paramedics are getting antsy with their stretcher but he needs to know, he needs it. *Just one minute, fellas, if you'd be so kind.*

The whole time he's been telling me this story something has been missing. Now I realize: no cough. He hasn't been awake this long without coughing in years.

All day, I've been hearing evidence—from doctors, nurses, Leslie. Evidence for optimism, evidence against. But this is all the evidence *I* need. He's going to die. That cough, his canary.

The saleswoman returns. Wouldn't you know it, there *is* a dead wasp!

Nice, he says. And allows himself finally to be shlepped away, the king on his litter.

Front of House

There are two Italian restaurants in this town. People come to Nora's, where I wait tables, when they can't get into the good one. This restaurant was bad long before I was hired, which somehow doesn't take any of the pressure off. When I make a mistake, I can feel Nora's eyes boring into me. She might correct me or, judging from her intensity, she might fight me. I consider her haircut, ostensibly a bob but with a lot of bourgeois suburbanite bells and whistles: chunky highlights, elaborate stacking up the back. I absolutely could not take her in a fight.

I'm not much of a waitress, it turns out. I struggle to remember which of Nora's essentially identical pasta dishes contain olives versus capers, pancetta versus prosciutto. My customers' appetizers routinely come at the same time as their mains. In the time it takes me to walk away from a table, I've already forgotten what they asked me for.

Wine is a particular headache—I don't drink it myself and my inexperience makes me clumsy with the wine key in front of customers. Nora watches me open bottles and, when her scrutiny makes my hands shake, she storms over to open them herself. Her face rabid, she pours my customers' wine gracefully and then slams the bottle down on their table. The slamming is her way of saying she'll cover my sorry ass this time but I'm in big trouble later, and she repeats it every time I get too nervous to open a bottle, which, before long, is every time. I get lavish pity tips whenever she puts on this terrifying show, so I can't say I mind it *that* much, though I do worry that one of these days, she's going to hit me.

She never hits me but she does throw a phone at me when I forget to pack a customer's complimentary side salad with the rest of his to-go order. Those damn salads—they come with every entrée but, because nobody actually eats those sad assemblages of elderly vegetables, they're the first thing we forget whenever we're in the weeds. The big black phone misses me, scuffing the wall behind me and startling the whole restaurant into silence. Nora doesn't look contrite as she sets the phone back in its cradle. At this point, it's well past time I regrouped.

"Let me have some of your Adderall," I say to the man who is still my husband. He prefers heroin to pills these days, and is therefore generous with his stash. God, I wish he would just let me go back to the strip club! I suppose I could get a job in a coffee shop instead—it's work I enjoy, and I can manage it without pills. But the money waiting tables is much closer to what I made in the club, and I've also become determined to prove to myself that I can do it.

My husband and I used to take Adderall together for fun, so I know what to expect: unnatural chattiness, equally unnatural ability to focus. Not only will I remember my customers' requests for once, but I'll have a great time doing it—plus all the side work for the whole restaurant, and then maybe my taxes and an essay on Kant.

The next day, I'm a machine, I'm a god. I'm the best server Nora's ever had. "Isn't this unexpected," she says cattily as I open every wine bottle with panache, my gestures as practiced and confident as if I had actually practiced them. I remember to recommend the pricier dishes and I know what ingredients are in them. Customers barely have a chance to sip their water before I appear, a phantasm with a sweating pitcher, to top them off. My pity tips are phased out, replaced by real ones.

It's a relief to finally have a decent day at work, beyond which relief I feel nothing. Taking care of these customers isn't even like taking care of people, frankly. These are spoiled pets, inexplicably dependent on me to feed them, and because they aren't cute like pets I feel mostly disdain for them. They speak, and as I write down their requests, I convert them, in my head, to numbers, which good servers know better than to do because the exercise is generally depressing and de-motivating. A nine-dollar glass of house red. A seventeen-dollar pasta to share. Zero dollars for dessert, they couldn't manage another bite. These particular pets might earn me a fiver. I yearn to wade through hundred-dollar bills again. I am working so diligently for so little reason.

The literature of the restaurant is concerned in large part with the artistry of food—with chefs' vision as creators, what distinguishes Anthony Bourdain's from Gabrielle Hamilton's. But there's much less literature dedicated to serving that artful food to people. My very scientific study of one bookstore's food-writing section reveals fifty books, mostly memoirs, zero of which are about the front of house even though those books do exist (Phoebe Damrosch's *Service Included: Four-Star Secrets of an Eavesdropping Waiter* comes to mind, as does Michael Cecchi-Azzolina's less good *Your Table Is Ready*). The job of hosts and servers is to set customers at ease, and we set them at ease by trying to seem like them, and I guess we've done so well at seeming like them that they've lost interest in what we do. So have many in the kitchen, for that matter, like petulant celebrity chef David Chang, who liked to tell his front-of-house staff that he could easily run a restaurant without them.

As Becca Schuh notes in her essay "Bad Waitress," self-styled intellectuals—even the ones who believe they're interested in great restaurants—tend to show a surprising lack of curiosity about the front-of-house workers in those restaurants, even though those are the ones who give diners the most direct time and attention. Maybe, because they have much more interaction with waitstaff than with chefs during their meals, they think they know how our servile illusions work, our naked upsellings of cheap bready appetizers, the suggestive way we slip them dessert menus whether they've asked for one or not. That, or they don't recognize the illusions, so seamlessly are they performed. Cooks can correctly argue that, if they didn't prepare the various crudos and pastas of a contemporary fine-dining menu, customers would have no way of eating them. There's real mystery to what they do. But serving? Carrying plates and filling water glasses? Customers do that at home. What's to know?

Will Guidara's *Unreasonable Hospitality* is probably the best-known recent nonfiction book that highlights, for a change, the

seriousness of front-of-house work. It even has a cameo on FX's
beloved restaurant dramedy *The Bear*—we see it inspire hapless,
beaten-down Richie to become the eponymous restaurant's
überwaiter. Problem is, Guidara is a *boss*, not a waiter. He used
to co-own about a half dozen high-end restaurants, including the
venerated Eleven Madison Park where *Unreasonable Hospitality*
spends most of its time. For all its fame, Guidara's book is not a
memoir of restaurant labor. It's a book for managers, using the
example of hospitality to open readers' eyes to what their busi-
nesses could be and what their workers could be pushed to do.

As such, the examples of hospitality that appear in books like
this are typically—to use Guidara's own term—unreasonable.
Only the most bombastic case studies will inspire managers to
dizzying new heights of, uh, management. At one of Union
Square Hospitality Group kingpin Danny Meyer's restaurants,
where Guidara got his start, a couple realize they've left a bottle
of champagne in their freezer, and their sommelier borrows
their house keys so he can rescue it for them before it explodes
without interrupting their anniversary dinner. When a Spanish family dining at Eleven Madison Park is enchanted by the
New York snowfall, Guidara sends a staff member to buy four
brand-new sleds and chauffeur the family to the park for an
impromptu sleigh ride. As Richie would say approvingly, that's
gangster. One does wonder, though, what it's like to be the guy
tasked with shlepping four sleds through a snowstorm, rather
than the guy who excitedly hatched the plan to buy them.

Books like *Unreasonable Hospitality* are for plan-hatchers more
than sled-shleppers. Me, I never cared enough about the work to

be more than a sled-shlepper, and I rarely got to work in places that would have asked their servers to shlep sleds anyway—there was too much other work to be done, and too few hands available to do it. In most restaurants I was server, busser, and host, three jobs that are explicitly for three separate people in places as high-end as Eleven Madison Park. I packed to-go orders and battled reservation management software, all while remembering who asked for wine and who needed ketchup, that horrible kitchen bell puncturing my every attempt to stay organized with yet another dish that needed running, always more, *always more,* something always forgotten.

It's not that servers in fine dining don't work hard; it's that their hard work looks elegant, while mine only ever looked hard. While working first at Nora's and later at similarly slapdash restaurants, I read everything I could find about these rarefied, regimented workplaces. I loved learning about this country that bordered the one I lived in but observed totally foreign customs. Where are the shitty side salads that nobody wants? The paper tablecloths with their radar maps of grease and mustard stains? Tell me again about this thing you call family meal where everybody sits down for a *whole dinner* at the *same time,* instead of stealing two minutes to deep-throat a KIND Bar. And don't leave anything out!

When I move to New York, I audition at one strip club that's an hour's train ride from my apartment and smells uncannily of barbecue ribs, which it doesn't serve. Do I really want to take an hour-long train ride home at 3 A.M. with hundreds of dollars of cash on my person six nights a week? I do not, so I grudgingly reenter the world of restaurant work instead. Grudgingly and slowly, I should say, since all the restaurants here want "New York experience" and it's tough to land a job. I'm reminded at every interview of the fable that the city's tap water imbues its bagels and pizzas with mystical properties. It must imbue its servers with something similar, something I don't have.

I never do wrangle a job waiting tables, but one restaurant with a Michelin star hires me to be a reservationist. Finally, a place among the regimented, artful people! Finally, a restaurant job that's only one job! The general manager, Gerard, who hires me is the type of man my husband Sean calls a "slick-dick mutherfucker," with his Tom Ford eyeglasses and slim-cut suit. Every gesture he makes looks simultaneously corny and cool, somehow—the mark of the fine-dining manager. He explains that this is the most romantic restaurant in New York and he, Gerard, plans to keep it that way. He explains this in a tone I've only ever heard commanding Chuck Heston to remove his shoes, for the place where he stands is holy ground. I try to look dazzled. Slick dick indeed.

The "office" where I take reservations is an unheated outbuilding. A team of florists uses it to assemble the restaurant's shocking daily floral bonanzas. I've never seen flowers in such quantities or forced into such ghastly shapes; when a florist finishes an arrangement, she struggles to lift it. A cat with a pendulous gut moseys about, supervising our work between vomits. Our two computers are about as old as computers can be and still run OpenTable, which we use to make and organize reservations. Thrillingly, there is family meal twice a day—one for the morning's prep staff, one for the evening's service staff. I grow cheerfully bloated on the line cooks' pasta bakes. So *this* is fine dining!

Most romantic restaurant in New York, says Gerard; maybe if you're ninety years old, says I. Our books are filled with surnames I last heard modified with "robber baron" in U.S. history class. To the power of these august names, even I with my general distaste for customers am not entirely immune. Many of our regulars have been dining here for thirty-five years, and they were already old then. This may be the only restaurant in New York whose VIPs clamor for five o'clock tables.

We in the office prefer when our customers' assistants make the reservations, as they're in roughly the same position we're in, job-wise, and are easier to deal with as a result. Some of these calls are pretty funny—a fine-dining reservationist and an assistant, each trying to out-help the other. *No, please, after you.* After assistants, people who have been saving up for this specific dinner for a long time are the most pleasant, followed in descending order by tourists (American), tourists (continental European), and wealthy locals. When friction happens, it's most often because every single person demands to sit next to the window, which has a pretty view of the river. Pretty, not extraordinary, and certainly not life-changing the way you'd think it was, considering the tenor of these requests.

"We are coming all the way from Italy to eat at your place, and you tell me you cannot honor one simple request?" says one irate customer.

"I'm asking my girlfriend to marry me at this dinner," says another. "I need that window table. You don't know what it's like."

"My grandmother was in the shipping industry," says my favorite one yet. "It comforts her to look at the water while she eats, and you want to take that away from her."

What I really wish I could say is that you're not sitting next to the window unless you are a literal Rockefeller. I'm not supposed to even make a note of these requests, since, again, *every single person* makes the same one. Some people pick real fights with me about this—screaming, insults, the works. One guy tries, belligerently, to bribe me. Mostly, it's just bog-standard customer bitching, to be tuned out and mocked later.

At Nora's restaurant, where the mood was that of underlings tiptoeing as quietly as possible around Hitler's bunker, it was hard to take any sort of pride in my work. It was hard enough to get through a shift without any violent incidents. Working for Gerard, I begin to see what service can be if I let it, if I slice a little vent in me through which my dignity can escape, the way my highest-earning coworkers have done. Customers' demands are in one sense annoying as shit, in another sense puzzles to be solved: *If I can't give you the window table, what can I give you?* I learn how to say no without using the word "no." I learn how to disguise it as an obsequious yes. I don't feel as if I'm answering the call of a hospitality tradition as ancient as guesthood itself, but if I can wrangle wins for a dozen difficult customers, I'm proud of myself a dozen times; that's something.

———

George Orwell's *Down and Out in Paris and London* does, unusually enough, take up the restaurant waiter as object of interest, but doesn't have anything nice to say about the poor guy. "He . . . is proud in a way of his skill, but his skill is chiefly in being servile," the author seethes. "His work gives him the mentality, not of a workman, but of a snob." Because of his proximity to the restaurant's wealthy patrons, Orwell theorizes, the waiter aspires solely and pridelessly to wealth, while cooks and chefs aspire to—here it is again—artistry. But they're not just artists. The cook is also identified by Orwell as the most workmanlike and least servile member of the restaurant's staff. He holds these traits at opposite ends of a spectrum: If you fall here, you are a strongman *and* an artiste; here, and you're an uppity brown-noser. You can be a relatively hardworking brown-noser, but, as Orwell himself sneers, "The moral is, never be sorry for a waiter." This book was published in 1933, and in the intervening ninety years, the moral hasn't changed much. Hateful stuff, but a stubborn ember of truth burns in it to this day.

An ugly suspicion I have is that intellectual types feel so romantic about chefs at least partly because they sense that working in a kitchen is dangerous, and painful, and hard on both body and spirit. Note that I say "chefs" and not "cooks" here (and certainly not "dishwashers," whom Orwell, too, sees as unskilled and pitiable). No matter how many *Kitchen Confidentials* and *Heats* explicitly say otherwise, these people persist in the belief that the glamorous chef-owner of some Michelin-starred bistro is cooking on the line every night, sweating his personal celebrity sweat into the food. That only adds to the romance—that someone both famous and brilliant would preside over smoky burners for fourteen hours a day in service to his calling. When the person destroying his body for food also has his name on the restaurant, it's admirable. When that person is some guy who's never been on Food Network and shares his outer-borough one-bedroom with four other people, it forces his would-be admirers to ask some difficult questions. Not everyone who cooks great art gets treated like a great artist.

We in the front of house have to ask ourselves similarly difficult questions. With his servile/workmanlike spectrum, Orwell seems to have spotted the seesaw nature of every restaurant shift—waitstaff on one end, kitchen staff on the other. When our end of the seesaw shoots up, thanks to a bustling dinner rush full of easy-to-upsell customers, the kitchen workers are forced to cook at warp speed for none of the tips that make all that rushing worth our while. When the rush dies and the workers in the kitchen can cook at a more manageable pace, we plummet, tipless and griping. There's tension, often. Screaming matches and stormings-out. I can't remember a single shift I've worked when front and back of house agreed on how good the night was. This dynamic puts us at odds with our colleagues in the kitchen, a routine death blow to the potential for professional solidarity between the front and back of house, as anonymous author prole.info notes in his pamphlet *Abolish Restaurants*. It's hard to feel good about being at odds with people who have to work much longer shifts than us for less money and (because so many kitchen staff are undocumented migrants) minimal workplace protections. But ultimately, in this conflict, everybody loses.

According to one study, line cooks saw a 60 percent increase in their mortality rate during the pandemic—higher than workers in any other job. Bakers are on the list, too, a few spots down from line cooks. Chefs and head cooks saw a smaller increase, and bartenders' was smaller still. Front-of-house staff don't appear on the list at all. No one study can say everything about every restaurant. There are so many reasons that we in the front of house did not die at the same rate as our comrades in the back—one possibility that comes to mind is that many restaurants closed their dining rooms at the height of the pandemic, but maintained a kitchen and bar for to-go orders. You don't take your life into your hands on the job if you don't have a job. Still, those numbers illustrate the most brutal division between front and back of house. We who serve might be abused by hateful customers that we cry about in the walk-in refrigerator, and they who cook might die.

We've all met them—the servers who drink the Kool-Aid. Let's call them Orwellian servers, the ones who come closest to proving that author's point about the money-hungry snobbery in the front of house. Even off the clock, Orwellian servers' conversation is all tasting notes and ingredient provenances. They drink the usual dive bar swill that restaurant workers can afford, but they swish it in their mouths before they swallow, maybe unconsciously, maybe hoping it looks like they're doing it unconsciously. Once they settle into a position of some influence at whatever fine-dining restaurant created their work persona, they never leave it. Those few restaurant groups that offer health insurance and paid time off—including, as it happens, Union Square Hospitality Group—they're *full* of Kool-Aid drinkers.

In *Sweetbitter,* Stephanie Danler's novel about waiting tables at a fictional version of Danny Meyer's Union Square Cafe, the Orwellian-in-chief is a server named Simone. It's hard to say how much of Simone's awfulness is Danler's fault versus how much of it is by Danler's design—should we be as spellbound by her as the narrator Tess is? She's remote and affected. She has the requisite obscure theories about wine and a close relationship with the manager. Like many fine-dining lifers, she harbors a Cinderella fantasy about her restaurant's wealthy patrons, one of whom may install her in his Connecticut estate and thus rescue her from a life of plate-bearing and crumb-scraping. She teaches Tess, in essence, how to be the sort of server for whom such a rescue is even a possibility: as identical to the customers as possible in sensibility, despite the fact that her work is what facilitates their play.

The Orwellian server par excellence in Merritt Tierce's novel *Love Me Back* is the high-grossing Cal, who keeps bags of coke and cigarettes in his work locker to pass on to "his people"—not family members or friends, of course, but VIP customers. Like every Orwellian server I've ever met, he believes fervently in manifesting success through the power of positive thinking. It always sounds like bullshit, but the other thing about these people is that a huge percentage of their tips are from parties who come to the restaurant specifically to be waited on by them, so you end up wondering if maybe they're onto something. As with Simone, Cal's success comes half from his ability to present himself to his customers as totally ego-free, and half from his massive ego.

I'm not allowed to wait tables while working for Gerard—in fact, I'm strongly discouraged from going anywhere near the dining room with my shaved head and tattooed arms. But I become, briefly and in a comparatively modest way, an Orwellian reservationist. I'm so proud of the restaurant's Michelin star that you'd think I single-handedly earned it. Joining my colleagues for family meal, I think *Look at us, eating together like a real family.* I would never be permitted to describe our food or wines to customers, but I study them anyway, just in case a caller has questions while making a reservation. Though my mind is brimming with lavish descriptions of every signature dish, the only question anyone ever asks me about our tasting menu is how much it costs.

Then one night it occurs to me that I'm shivering. Winter has blown in and stripped my bootleg office of both light and warmth. The florists clock out for the day, leaving me alone in a dark little hut with only the light of my computer to see by. If I wedge the space heater between my legs, I can just about stop losing warmth, but I can't get any. Making reservations, my primary job and one in which I've begun to take real pride, becomes nearly impossible. The only thing harder than holding a phone in a numb and icy hand is typing on OpenTable with it.

"Th-th-th-thank you for c-c-calling," I say, hating myself for my chattering teeth and my total lack of toughness. "Wh-wh-what can I do for you?"

Oh. Right. This is the virtuous work of hospitality, but it's also poorly compensated wage labor that does not, strictly speaking, need to be done. It's a realization that strikes every Orwellian server eventually. The ones you meet in their final form—the ones who have spent decades at the restaurant where you, starry-eyed and green, just got hired; they've smothered that realization under so many layers of either pride or pretension that it rarely bubbles up to the surface anymore. Turning blue in that office, I can't smother it. It isn't the worst thing that's ever happened to me at a restaurant job, but it's somehow the hardest to bear. I've set a pat of butter on my space heater to soften so I can distract myself with a buttered roll, and the room is so cold that it won't melt. I try to load YouTube on the ancient computer, just to distract myself between calls, and find that Gerard has put a blocker on the site, along with most others that aren't OpenTable or Gmail. I amuse myself by reorganizing our OpenTable reservations first by name and then by confirmation status for three minutes, which is exactly how many minutes it's possible to amuse one's self in this way. So it's to be this, then—just me and my pride, whatever I can summon up of it to keep me company. After it feels like an hour has passed, I allow myself a glance at the computer's clock. Ah. Seven minutes.

By the end of *Sweetbitter,* Simone has forced Tess out of the restaurant, the way any Orwellian server worth her tips can do with any underling she dislikes. On her way out, Tess muses on why the restaurant asks for so much more than mere work from its workers—why they're also expected to care, to take ownership, to be a family, however dysfunctional. In the book's truest moment, Tess realizes how little all that devotion ultimately means, how unstable a structure it's built for her to live in. "They would miss me for a week," she thinks. "At most."

I end up quitting based on roughly the same realization. They were never going to let me in that dining room, with all my memorizations that nobody asked me for. I get a different job, one of the thousands of readily gettable jobs there are in this city, in a place with no fine-dining aspirations but fully functional central heat and AC. I don't need work to be my art or my pride. I need a job to pay me my money every two weeks, and to be tolerable—that's all.

About a year after the publication of *Tacky* and six months after getting sober, I realize I'm running out of money. I should have gotten sober a few thousand dollars' worth of cocaine ago.

I'm a professional writer now, and have been for some time. I could try to make money in writerly ways if I wanted. But why would I freelance for money I need *now*—especially when each freelancing gig earns me about three hundred dollars before tax? I know a much faster and more reliable way to make three hundred dollars, and it doesn't even entail writing any emails whose subject line is "Just following up :)". I respond to some Craigslist ads and find a hosting job in a restaurant faster than I'd be able to get an email back from most magazines' billing departments.

The irony is that, a decade post-Nora, I have a prescription for a different ADHD medication, one obtained honorably. But because hosting at the restaurant is my second job, which I do at night after a full day of writing, the meds start leaving my system around the time that I'm clocking in for my shift. I suppose I could just take more, but I no longer have it in me to come down from stimulants at three in the morning. Sober, there's a lot that I no longer have in me—including, as it happens, restaurant work.

It's the most darling place, the bistro where I'm working. Warmly dark, warmly cramped, like sitting around a roaring campfire in a cave. Most of our regular customers are men who show up with a new date every night, all of whom fawn over the restaurant's elegance. Our cocktails look delectable, each one a different jewel tone with something tasty and caramelized bobbing around in it. The food is small but scrumptious, so that our customers typically order huge amounts of it. Servers don't have to work all that hard on their customers to rack up a stratospheric bill, off which we all stand to earn stratospheric tips, even me.

I like my coworkers and I want to do the place proud, but I haven't improved at restaurant work in the years since I quit doing it. And it's not like I spent those years training my memory palace with brain exercises—I've been battering myself with drugs this whole time. Even hosting, a less mentally taxing job than waiting tables, is too much for me now. Customers have this pesky habit of wanting to know how long it'll be before their table is ready. I don't know that because no one could ever know that. I give them my best guess, which is often wrong. People are eager to complain that I told them it would be thirty minutes thirty-two minutes ago. I develop a new forehead wrinkle and a thin layer of stress acne.

A couple times, customers recognize me from Twitter or my author photo, and some of those customers are even kind enough to act starry-eyed. The best one is the woman who was reading my book on the very train she took to get here. I sign it for her. In my inscription, I recommend the scallop fritters.

The guy waiting in line behind her asks me what that was about, his tone suggesting that he's caught me doing something wrong.

"I was just signing her book," I said, newly self-conscious. "I mean, *my* book. Or it's hers, only . . . I wrote it. I'm a writer."

It is, by far, the clumsiest way anyone has ever said "I was signing her copy of the book I wrote." But his tone made me want to defend myself, which is not something I'm really allowed to do with a customer. His expression doesn't improve any as he absorbs my explanation. *Here you are,* his face seems to say, *a hostess in the restaurant where people like me pay to eat, acting like some kind of celebrity.*

After I lead him to a much worse table than I'd initially planned to seat him at, I look up his name and learn that his job is something called "manager of digital optimization analytics." Oh, customers.

In this job, I often feel like I'm back in Nora's restaurant in the days before the Adderall, minus the fear that I'm about to be assaulted. Actually, it's almost worse that my gentle manager would never hit me—when I drop a customer's toasted ciabatta in her lap, I'd rather get whacked in the head about it than just stand there feeling stupid. One night, our chef offhandedly tells me that I'm the least important element of this restaurant's operation. There was a time when that would have hurt my feelings. Now it only makes me say *Okay, can I clock out early, then?* I've become Mrs. Can I Clock Out Early. Gerard took me to a fork in the road, showing me what a career in hospitality could feel like; I took the other fork long ago, and there's no going back to the bud of shy pride I left to wither.

I quit the bistro when I sell this very book. I started working there because I needed fast money, but also, if I'm honest with myself, because I imagined a redemption arc: Rax conquers the front of house. I pictured myself sailing from table to table with trays lining both my arms and my customers' requests all firmly in my head. In my dreams, I told parties of two that their tables would be ready in thirty minutes and seated them in twenty-five. The place would be sparkling, thanks to me, and every dish would taste divine. Perfection, that's what I was after, and nothing less.

I never got there. I never even had one perfect shift. The closest I get to all that glory is when the woman whose book I signed stops at the host stand on her way out the door. "You were right about the fritters. I've never even tried scallops before tonight," she says.

On my last night, instead of fulfilling my dreams of triumph, I content myself with doing a mammoth amount of side work. I swaddle every piece of silverware we have in napkins for the customers, including the forks my manager had set aside for us to use at family meal later; no matter, they're mine now, and rolled up beautifully. I fill two pitchers with espresso for espresso martinis, which our customers adore in direct proportion to how obnoxious they are to make. Then I deep clean the espresso machine and, finally, everything else I can find. I go through a dozen rags and half a bottle of Fabuloso. No one else can find any rags. Tough shit—tonight, these people are dining in *my* house, and my house *will* be spotless. In my mania for cleaning and prepping, I'm exorcising a demon: Rax the waitress, Rax the hostess, Rax the lousy restaurant worker with a chip on her shoulder.

When I clock out for the last time, I give my manager an epic poem's worth of description of every task I've accomplished on this night.

"Thanks," she says. When she sees that I'm waiting for a more epic response, she adds, "Thanks so much."

Bad Friend

When I graduated from college, I lived for a time in one of those "luxury apartments" in D.C. that I'm sure *would* have been luxurious had its dwellers been the laughing, upwardly mobile couple from the building's advertising. True, the one-bedroom I shared with my roommates was massive and included such frivolous rooms as "sunroom" and "study." In practice, though, every room of our apartment was a bedroom. Mine was the sunroom-bedroom, with floor-to-ceiling windows for walls and a sliding glass door for egress. It offered neither heat, nor privacy, nor space.

I paid nine hundred dollars a month to shiver in that sunroom and politely avoid my roommates, who returned the favor. Its cramped chill made it the least livable room in the place, but not by much—Nelson paid a hundred more than I did for more space and privacy but no windows. Only Roger and Mandy, who had moved in first and therefore had the privilege of claiming the master bedroom, could live as breezily as the couple from the building's brochures did. Open-mouthed laughter seemed to be a prerequisite of the lifestyle. They laughed over red wine at the kitchen bar and laughed over goat cheese salads at the dining room table. Then they showered laughingly together in the master bathroom and, presumably, laughed themselves to sleep at night, comfortable in a way that Nelson and I couldn't be for much less money.

It was the most conveniently located apartment I could afford, so there was no point in complaining. I wouldn't have even known about the room if not for Nelson, who at that time was something like my friend. We drank together, most often in a silence that drove me bananas. It was better than drinking alone, I told myself, occasionally through gritted teeth. Nelson was a reserved guy, quiet by nature, and so we would pursue our respective intoxications while I tried like hell to draw him out. It wasn't that I was so desperate to converse with Nelson specifically, who in the few years I knew him could only be counted on to show genuine enthusiasm for golf. We had nothing in common, and he was right that shared, silent drunkenness was the most rewarding use of our time together. But it embarrassed me to sit in public so unsociably. Every time we got together, I asked him about everything I could think of—his job, his parents, his love life (in the form of his equally laconic girlfriend, Shauna). Such was my mania to make a conversation, any conversation, happen. Then one day, I happened to ask about his apartment, and that's how I came to live in the least comfortable room of it for six months. It was our most productive conversation ever.

Because I, like most addicts, am dangerously self-obsessed, I have a hard time with friendships. Making a friend relies in large part on one's ability to pay attention to others, not historically one of my strengths. The tooth-gnashing awkwardness of my silent outings with Nelson would have been more tolerable if other variants on that awkwardness weren't already so familiar to me. I'd convinced myself that the issue wasn't his and my fundamental incompatibility, but *my* fundamental incompatibility, with *everyone*. I never knew what to say. It didn't matter who I was with, how close I believed we were—I did not, under any circumstances, know what to say. If I said what was on my mind, I would have spent most friendly get-togethers weeping over how I wished I'd never been born, a behavior that tends to steal focus. If anything, Nelson made things easier because our awkwardness felt refreshingly like a specific problem I could try to solve, rather than an a priori condition of being alive.

But even with friends who were less opposed to the art of conversation than Nelson was, the terrible moment always came, after the exchanging of pleasantries and the asking-after of loved ones, when we would fall into quiet. If we were at a restaurant, I could usually pretend that I'd implemented this quiet on purpose so I could review the menu or eat my meal. In other places, there might be an interesting graffitus on the wall or a man muttering creepily to himself, some damn thing, anything I could incorporate into a new stage of conversation. Other times, I could only berate myself: *Say something! Do something! If this friendship disintegrates after today, it will be your fault!*

"It's so nice to see you," my friend might say at some point, blithely unaware that this had become another worst day of my life. "It's been too long!"

"It has," I'd agree while promising myself that I would never try to socialize with this person, or indeed any person, again.

———

I spent my first few years on the planet blissfully unaware of how fucking difficult friendship is, but all that changed in second grade, when I met Amelia.

The key to Amelia's appeal was in her head of shining golden hair. It's hard to overstate the power shining golden hair had over all of us in the '90s—I believe it made me fall so completely under Amelia's spell that, even now, it's tough to pinpoint when I should have started putting my guard up. When she stole my glasses for a full day, preventing me from doing my schoolwork and getting me in trouble? When she kept asking me about blow jobs during Two Truths and a Lie to get a laugh out of the boys, even though I didn't know what a blow job was and I suspect neither did she? When we pretended to be the Spice Girls and she insisted on always playing Posh Spice despite the fact that *I was the one with fucking brown hair, Amelia?*

Amelia wasn't evil—just a wuss. Her other friends were the Girls, our school's fledgling social dictators and future MLM saleswomen, five wispy blondes and a token Jew. The first time I visited Amelia's McMansion, I saw a photo of the Girls' mothers lined up prom-night-style with their husbands' arms around their pregnant bellies. Even before they were born, the Girls spent every minute together. (My mother recently told me that Amelia's mother used to call her up, ostensibly to coordinate our plans but really to ply her for information about how little money we had compared to her and her husband. "I guess it made her feel better about herself," she said, which led me to believe that, whatever Amelia was, at least she came by it honestly.)

Amelia expected of herself what the Girls expected of her, had most of her thoughts using their shared brain. These weren't the only thoughts she had but, amplified by five imperious other voices, they were the loudest.

One day, she called me her best friend and then froze. "If you *ever* tell anyone I said that, I'll pummel your *ass.*"

"I won't," I said, happiness melting my insides. "I promise." And I never did until now, maybe because I felt smug that "ass" was a word she'd learned from me.

I couldn't quite believe in her cruelty towards me, even as it mounted, day after day. She only performed it when the Girls were around, which made it feel unreal and theatrical, a part she was playing in a vaudeville show. Being her victim felt more like being her straight man—the less fun lead to play, but still a lead. Then, too, friendship with her was such a rollicking adventure that I hated to ask questions about it. She was a despot, but a charismatic one. She always had a scheme for us. We played out the entire best friends montage for two years: Here we are writing short stories together about a superhero named Princess Amelia Raxington. Cut to us slathering raw egg masks on each other's faces and squealing at the stickiness. Now here we are practicing the choreography from *NSYNC's "Bye, Bye, Bye" video. And now it's my ninth birthday.

My mistake was inviting one of the other Girls to my party along with Amelia, who probably would have managed to loosen up if she didn't have to play to her usual audience. All we were doing was ordering pizza and watching *The Princess Bride*—there was no need to put on a show for *my* friends. But as it was, she must have felt she had no choice but to reprise her daily production, *She's Just So Annoying.*

For that's what I woke up to around one A.M.: Amelia saying in a low but authoritative voice, "She's just so *annoying.*"

"For sure," said Miriam, the other Girl I'd invited.

"Like, sitting there at recess, writing dumb little stories. Wearing clothes her mommy picked out. Barf."

It took me a minute to realize they were talking about me.

One by one, every friend I'd invited to celebrate my birthday agreed that I was annoying, and wrote dumb little stories, and dressed like a dork. They even managed to unanimously agree that *The Princess Bride* was stupid, though it had had us all in stitches just a few short hours before. I could understand why they were all shitting on me, as excruciating as it was. But what did William Goldman ever do to them?

I shriveled like a salted slug. Amelia's betrayal hurt, but it, at least, was predictable. The uninterested way Miriam agreed with her, as if I wasn't even worth the gossip, hurt a bit more. But my other friends had truly wounded me. I'd never doubted their warm feelings towards me until now, listening to them merrily deconstruct my flaws.

Only one girl piped up in my defense. "*I* like Rax," she said. "And I thought the movie was funny."

"I'm awake," I said then, terrified of what the others would fire back in response to her.

Everyone guiltily apologized to me, and I told them all I forgave them, sensing that this was the closest I could come to pretending it had only been a bad dream. What's more, from then on, I courted all those people more aggressively than ever before, even the friends whose companionship I'd never had to work for. The realization that I had to win their affection was enough to convince me that it was a prize.

As for the girl who stuck up for me, the only friend who made it clear that night that I could count on her, I can't even remember her name.

Crushingly lonely though I often was after that birthday party, I couldn't take much pleasure in the company of anyone who wanted to spend time with me. Their sincere affection for me poisoned their character and their judgment, as far as I was concerned. People who didn't like me would be more suitable friends, once I managed to win them over. (I look back at this juggling act of self-sabotage now and think: Jesus *Christ*! How did I ever have the energy for this?)

My friendship with Nelson was the perfect example of a difficult relationship that was also low stakes. Not everyone could be an Amelia, full of charisma and awfulness in perfectly equal proportions. Nelson was as responsive to my desperate gambits as lichen on a log, but at least I didn't love him enough for his quiet distance to wound me—not until the night I met him at our watering hole for what I figured would be our standard few hours of silence.

I met Nelson at his usual barstool, or at least that's who I thought I'd made plans to meet. My date for the evening certainly looked like Nelson. He was drinking one of Nelson's beloved Miller Lites, and Nelson's beat-up denim jacket hung off the back of his stool. Everything appeared to be in order, only . . . this guy threw his arms around me with gusto when he saw me, something Nelson would never do, except *maybe* on a

High Holy Day (opening day of the Masters Tournament or his mother's birthday). This man even greeted his girlfriend with a Christian side-hug. What was going on?

"Wow," I said, dazed and unprepared. "Hello to you, too, buddy!"

"Hey, brother!" he said. I registered the moment's importance: I was now, inexplicably, *brother*. "Glad you made it. Pop a squat."

"Did you just tell me to 'pop a squat'?" I asked, doing so.

I'd never seen Nelson like this: animated, chatty, without even being drunk. His speech was as swift and clear as a college debater's, as opposed to the way his speech normally was, which was nonexistent. Presently he offered me a leather coin purse. Take it to the bathroom, he said. All will be revealed in the bathroom.

I accepted this without question. All was so often revealed in the bathroom. There, in a stall, I found an eight ball in the coin purse.

Of course. Only cocaine could make Nelson think it was a good idea to hold me close and call me "brother." Far from feeling disappointed that his sudden enthusiasm for my company was due to a drug, I was encouraged. What was I if not Diet Nelson, as awkward and quiet as he was at heart, just more inclined to hide it? If coke could bring out his pop-a-squat-brother side, I couldn't wait to see what it did for me.

I finished powdering my nose and left the bathroom to find Nelson deep in conversation with the bartender, a situation that would have normally paralyzed me. I hated when my friends invited me out and then had the nerve to talk to people I didn't know, as if they didn't realize I'd been planning to hoard their attention for myself. Tonight, though, was different. For once, I believed in my ability to talk to strangers.

For the next hour, Nelson and I worked the room, trading his coin purse back and forth whenever it seemed like one of us might be floating back down to earth. I didn't know any of the people in this bar, and he didn't seem to either, but for the first time in both our lives we had something to say. No, we had everything to say. I sidled up to a table where two guys were arguing about which Clash album was the best, which as it happened was one of my areas of expertise. I sat down with them (God, did I really?) and made my case, at some length, for a tie between their self-titled debut and *Sandinista!* I had less expertise to contribute to their ensuing discussion of the 1992 Olympics, but having nothing substantive to add didn't bother me. I was victimizing these two guys with my epiphany that it didn't matter whether I had anything substantive to add to a discussion; it was enough to add enthusiasm. Enthusiasm for life, for my new friends, for enthusiasm itself. That's all cocaine is, really—an enthusiasm-seeking missile. Allow it access to your brain, and it will convince you that merely by virtue of being one of God's creatures, you know more than you think you do about the Dream Team.

"Oh, *shit*," said Nelson, leaning against my chair. The guys I was sitting with looked pained. Cokeheads are an exponential burden on a pleasant evening. You might add one to your conversation without sacrificing your good time entirely, but two cokeheads will ruin your night, and three or more will ruin your credit. "I know you're not over here talking about my man Scottie Pippen without me!"

"Uh, yeah," said Blond Guy.

"Oh, *shit*! The legend himself! O King of Kings! When I tell you all right now that Scottie mutherfucking Pippen is my king!" Standing there, with the three of us looking up at him from our chairs, Nelson resembled nothing more in that moment than Mussolini holding forth from the balcony.

"Isn't the King of Kings, like . . . Jesus?" asked Black-Haired Guy.

"For sure," Nelson said. He cast a pious glance skyward, paying tribute to, like, Jesus.

Thank God Nelson offered the guys his coke. He must have already known, and I would soon learn, that the only way to avoid hating yourself for acting like an asshole while on coke is to make accomplices of the people witnessing your behavior. After their trip to the bathroom with the coin purse, the two guys finally revealed to me that they were Adam and Marcus. They apologized for freezing me out earlier, even though that was an entirely reasonable thing to do, and even though I had been too full of coked-up bluster to notice—in any event, Adam and Marcus were now ready to welcome me and Nelson into their night, which would no longer be devoted to the Clash or the Dream Team, but to the pursuit of ingesting as much cocaine as possible.

We made quick work of that eight ball and suddenly I had three new best friends hanging on my every word. Nelson found more coke, and with more coke came more new friends. Had friendship been so easy this entire time? I felt like a video game character who'd finally equipped the right weapon to defeat a difficult boss. Sober, I wasted all my thoughts on my own brain, where they could not dazzle; high, I said every thought as soon as it crept into my head, and this crowd couldn't get enough, and didn't respond to the things I said, exactly, because they had too many of their own thoughts to fire into the air, but still the mood was genial as we absorbed each other's brains and decided we all loved each other. We all loved each other *so much*.

Cocaine took most of the friction out of the difficult friendships I had come to need. With coke on my side, the only remotely tricky step was getting some acquaintance to do it with me. I still had to work for their love, but when the drug was in my system I also knew I'd win it. I could tell I'd hit my target when the person I hoped to seduce into friendship got high enough to say:

"You know, Rax, I always thought you were kind of a bitch. But actually, you're really cool!"

More than the drug itself, *this* is what I got addicted to— the sense that the coke I offered people would set the record straight. I rarely wasted a coke binge on people who already loved me. The drug told the exact story I'd long hoped to be able to tell about my friendship, which is that it was worth something, dammit, and had been right there under your nose all along.

At my father's funeral, his friends spoke about his cheerfulness, his humor, his seemingly endless reserves of energy. They meant what they said, but they couldn't have been more wrong.

The only speaker who described a man I recognized was my father's best friend, Daniel, whom he'd met in rehab in the '80s. Daniel had been an Olympic-qualifying swimmer in his youth, dangerously handsome, a hellion; he now had Stage 4 esophageal cancer and needed to be escorted to the front of the room. There, he leaned against the mantel and shone a benevolent smile on us all.

"He was not a happy guy," Daniel said. "I knew him forty years, mostly from our bitter chess rivalry." Titters from the gathered listeners, many of whom had shared their own bitter chess rivalries with my father. "He would have loved hearing that none of you ever knew how sad he was. I wish he'd loved himself like all of us loved him. I wish he'd known how many people saw him as the guy he never knew how to be."

I sought out Daniel after his speech. "Would've been nice to meet this cheerful, easygoing guy that everyone else has been talking about all night," I said. "He would've been a great dad."

"Don't hold it against them," he said, waving a hand to indicate the others in the room. "These were people he always wanted to impress."

All at once, the reality of my father's friendships—the longevity of which had always been a source of immense pride for him—hit me in a new way. I took in his well-dressed friends, all wealthier and more professionally successful than he'd ever been. Most of them were heavy drinkers, Daniel being the only still-living sober buddy that my father had left. The room had an appealing wine cellar smell to it, dankly sophisticated—only a rich person's house can stink in a way that's sexy rather than just sad. I saw what my father must have seen during his decades of gathering with these people: a roomful of glittering socialites who, if he could only impress them somehow, would serve as proof of his worth. He'd worked and worked to make them love him, and because he'd been working so hard that whole time, they hadn't even known him.

I am trying not to be like this. I catch myself mired in it all the time. At my funeral, I worry that there will be just as many people glittering like my father's friends did, tearfully eulogizing a person who never existed, because I never felt safe enough to introduce them to the one who does.

For six months Nelson and I lived together in this tetchy equilibrium: when we were high, we adored each other; when we were sober, we hated ourselves for the ludicrous ways we behaved while high. We had to confront the daily gap between what the coke said through our mouths and what we actually felt for each other, which was nothing. This was the most casual of drinking-buddies relationships, and when we weren't high we both knew it. But cocaine doesn't allow any relationship to be casual.

When describing their cocaine addictions, people often ask, rhetorically, where the money went. Well, I find the money easy enough to account for, but where did the friendship go? The talk, the affection? I believed I loved all the people who populated my coked-up benders, even the ones who only listened to my babbling because they were cornered. They, and I, seemed in those moments to exist in some grand humane harmony that I'd never believed in before. Where did all that harmony go?

It's a tough question to answer generally, but in the case of

Nelson it's pretty obvious where the love went: I was stealing from him the whole time we lived together. Not money, pills. He'd had surgery some years ago, for which he'd been prescribed way more Percocet than he needed for his recovery. He kept that Percocet in the medicine cabinet of our bathroom, which bathroom I'll remind you he was sharing with three other people. I don't know about you, but the first thing I do when confronted with a new bathroom is snoop in the medicine cabinet, even now that I don't do drugs anymore. Maybe he was a truly decent person, or a naive one, or a careless one. Maybe all three. After all, I hardly knew him.

I didn't take any Percocets the first time I encountered them in our bathroom, but I did gingerly remove the bottle from the cabinet and count the number of pills inside. He'd been prescribed thirty; twenty-seven were left. *Interesting,* I thought, making sure to replace the bottle at the correct angle and to close the cabinet door silently.

Later that day, when Nelson and I were sitting on the sofa together, I steered the "conversation" (meaning, my mostly unanswered conversational gambits) towards medical procedures. Have any interesting ones lately?

"Nah," he said, belching some eau de Miller Lite into the air.

I see. No medical procedures lately, then. No surgeries.

"Nah."

That means no injuries, I guess. No bum shoulders or impacted wisdom teeth.

"Nah."

He wasn't picking up what I was putting down, which makes

sense, in retrospect, because I had Percocet on the brain and was being conversationally insane. Okay. Fine. No bad shoulders, no dental problems, no torn ACLs—

"Yo, I did tear my ACL actually. Like ten years ago, right after I enlisted."

Ugh, this guy's a fucking *veteran?* I had few hang-ups about behaving like a scumbag, broadly speaking, but even I hesitated to steal pain meds from a veteran who had injured himself in the line of duty. It was a little too "B-plot on a not-very-good episode of *Shameless*" to even consider. I could have figured out a way to justify it on anti-imperialist grounds, but that sounded like a lot of work to me. So I dropped my interrogation, but he was into it now.

"Yeah, it was this crazy football thing. Took me out for months, I couldn't do shit. Ended up getting discharged before basic even started. My leg was never the same. Huge bummer, man."

"So no army for you," I said, my mouth watering.

"Sucks, right?"

"It *completely* sucks." I patted his shoulder. I must have been smiling so, so evilly. "Every man should have the opportunity to serve his country."

He might not have noticed my subsequent thieving if I hadn't taken every last pill out of that bottle before we all went our separate ways. Leaseholder Roger's lease was up, and he and Mandy had bought a new place, where as far as I know they're laughing over salads to this day. They moved first, leaving me and Nelson alone in their old apartment for a week. I was packing my books when he called for me from the bathroom.

"I'm missing something," he said, his expression disappointed. Too late, I put up my guard.

"Oh yeah? What's that?"

He didn't answer. Just kept his gaze steady for one, two, three seconds while I tried not to squirm. I reminded myself that the culprit could have been Roger or Mandy for all he knew, or, hell, one of the many Tinder dates I'd triaged through that apartment over the past six months. But there's no fooling people you do drugs with. They've seen you at your shadiest; they know what you're capable of. I'm sure he was thinking, too, that he would have shared his pills with me if I had asked. If I had trusted in his friendship that much. I could see it dawn on him that our relationship was a broken-down engine in the yard. I would never stop tinkering with it, and so it would never get the chance to work.

"Never mind," he said. He dropped his gaze. "I'm sure it'll turn up."

Later that night, I saw the orange Percocet bottle in the trash. I had ludicrously put it back in its spot in the cabinet after draining its contents, believing that would buy me . . . something. The benefit of the doubt, I suppose. Which, of course, I didn't deserve.

Did getting sober make me a better friend?

Yes, duh, of course, but also it sort of didn't. On the one hand, I would never strong-arm some guy into being my friend just so I'd have someone to drink with, only to steal that same guy's pain medication and lie about whether I'd done it. When I reduce my relationship with Nelson to that single sentence, it makes me seem cartoonishly evil, and it's a relief to be able to say that at least the cartoonishness belonged to the drugs and the alcohol, even if they didn't take all my evil with them when they left. But am I still self-obsessed? Do I still worry to an absurd degree about whether my loved ones hate me? Yes on both counts, and I don't know how good of a friend I can be when those qualities are in play.

After I gave up cocaine, I could no longer trust any of the progress it had convinced me I'd made. It had introduced a parasite into my sense of self, one I needed to kill before I could move forward with my social anxiety renewed and augmented. The problem wasn't just that I had to start over; it's that I had to start *all the way* over, as that teary-eyed birthday girl hiding her teddy bear at the bottom of her sleeping bag so her "best friend" doesn't mock her for having it. I got into the habit of blaming cocaine for moments of personal dysfunction that it was in no way responsible for—one example that comes to mind is the collapse of a friendship that ended not because of my coke addiction, but because I had been stealing all my friend's pain medication. Cocaine was a convincing scapegoat. It had made me an obnoxious, hypersocial loudmouth, to be sure, but it hadn't made me a liar or a thief.

The other night, I was waiting in line to use a restaurant's single-stall bathroom. There were three people in line ahead of me, and we'd all been waiting several minutes in a state of increasing agitation. The problem became apparent when the stall finally freed up: three girls had been in there, and it was obvious from their noisily inane chattering that they'd been doing coke.

Now, I'm no blushing virgin about drugs, but I do have some standards. The most important one is: you do not make a whole girls' trip out of your key bumps when the venue only has one single-stall bathroom. Each girl must use the stall separately and do her bumps quickly. A true lady will let other bathroom-seekers go ahead of her in such a situation, but that's going above and beyond the call of duty. Either way, this is no time to get sucked into those Clash-and-Dream-Team babblings that ate up so many years of my life. Even at my druggiest, I would *never* have shown that little respect for my fellow man. I would use him for his apartment, I would steal from him, but I wouldn't prevent him from relieving his bladder.

What I did to Nelson was much worse than what those annoying girls did to me, and knowing that I'd never do it again doesn't change that. Still, it's nice to remember that I did it before I bothered setting limits at all, before I fully considered that badness was something I could do and not just something that others did to me. That doesn't do poor stolen-from Nelson any good all these years later, but it's a relief to me. It seems that inconveniencing a line full of strangers is my limit, the thing I wouldn't do to other people even if I relapse tomorrow. It's not a virtuous person's limit, nor a particularly logical one. It's just the one I happened to stumble into first.

Up from Sloth

Recently, I spent three weeks plagued by a burning pain in my left shoulder. I sighed around the apartment, groaning importantly every time I had to adjust my back, until Sean couldn't take it anymore and made me go to the doctor. My husband is your average maddeningly healthy adult man who would try to put Neosporin over an exposed bone, so for *him* to make *me* seek medical care was sobering. As my appointment date approached, I imagined my doctor's grave face giving me the news. "It's Lou Gehrig's disease of the shoulder," she'd say. "I've never seen anything like it."

Inexplicably, she didn't diagnose me with Rax King's Lou Gehrig's Disease. Instead, she sent me to the one physical therapist in my insurance's network. His office looked like a not very challenging gym, every corner packed with grim-faced people on treadmills or arm bikes. The therapist himself was a garrulous chap in cargo shorts who began our visit with a riddle.

"Which is harder, sitting or standing?" he asked, rotating my arm in its socket.

"Uh, standing?"

"Ha!" he crowed. "Wrong! Sitting's *much* harder. I bet you're a writer, eh? And you write from home?"

I nodded, casting furtive glances at the other people in the office. Most of them were either very old or wearing the uniforms of hard physical work. I wasn't necessarily dying to admit, in this company, that I was a *writer*. A soft-handed little *typer*.

"You writers, you've all got the same trouble," said the therapist. "You're all hunching over your laptops in bed. Straining your backs and shoulders."

So the official diagnosis was that I was medically bad at being on the computer. Embarrassing, but not shocking, since I've always been one of the least athletic people on the planet. No wonder writing in bed—not one of life's more strenuous tasks— had knocked me on my ass. Every physical thing, I reflected philosophically as the doctor futzed with my arm, knocked me on my ass. I'd spent thirty-two years denying my body the right to thrive, and it had finally begun fighting back.

I should clarify before I continue that I'm unathletic, yes, but *not* a klutz. Mindy Kaling once noted that, when a romantic comedy wants its slender, beautiful protagonist to seem more relatable, it burdens her with the gracelessness of a wounded manatee. Any real woman who was as clumsy as a rom-com heroine would spend the bulk of her life in traction, but in the movies, "clumsy" is shorthand for "adorable." I cannot stress enough that I am not being adorable at you. While walking up a staircase or carrying a package, my limbs pretty much do what I ask them to do. Then I politely suggest that they might behave just as nicely for me during a game of H-O-R-S-E, and they go on strike: Not our jurisdiction, boss, but good luck to you.

I can hear a shuffling, a fell whisper, the sound of a thousand tiresome people lining up with their little suggestions. Have I tried a strengthening regimen? Zumba? Pilates? Do I know about women-only gyms, and might I feel more comfortable learning to work out there? Am I into pickleball? Would I like to join a really chill kickball league, literally no pressure? In short, have I heard the good news about our Lord and Savior, physical fitness?

These suggestions all come from people who swear they were once *just like me*. Who used to think they didn't have an athletic bone in their bodies, either, until they found whatever miracle sport or class they found. They're sincere, these Good Samaritans, often unsettlingly so. They're ill-equipped to hear me when I say that I really, really do not have an athletic bone in my body, and if I try any of the crap they suggest, I'm liable to break a bunch of the bones I do have.

I was no more athletic as a kid than I am now, but I wasn't outright hostile towards sports, either. I still believed I was on the verge of discovering the one that I was naturally gifted at. The "naturally gifted" part was important—there would be no 4 A.M. trainings in my future. I would be a prodigy or I would be nothing. My ambitions were cruelly abetted by popular movies of the day like *Remember the Titans* and *Bend It Like Beckham*. The former film revealed that sports were the cornerstone of a fulfilling life; when I skeptically asked whether that was true for girls, too, in swooped the latter with a boisterous *Yes!* And so, every time a sport failed to fulfill my life, I worried a little more, until the fateful day in sixth grade that still replays regularly in my nightmares.

My entire class was lined up on the playground to take turns hitting a softball with Mr. Pyle's bat. Mr. Pyle was our gym teacher and he was a mean, mean old cuss—whoever first said people mellow with age had clearly never taken his class. His habit was to take a power stance, legs apart, arms crossed, whistle hanging loosely between his lips like a cigarette might have done in a more laid-back person's mouth. Thus positioned, he waited for one of us (usually me) to commit an error so that he could rapidly suck the whistle into position and—*CHEEP! CHEEP! CHEEP!* "Do it again, Rax!" It's been twenty years since I took his class and I still sometimes Google his name when I'm feeling down, hoping for a pick-me-up in the form of his obituary.

Let's speed-run this part, because thinking about it is giving me reflux: I didn't hit the damn ball, *obviously*. Didn't get within a yard of it. Other students had failed too, and Mr. Pyle had barked at each one about how the important thing was that they'd tried their best, but I was the only one who'd failed just as resoundingly at every other task he'd ever assigned. He must have thought I was fucking with him at that point. His words of consolation for me were a little different.

"JESUS CHRIST, YOU'RE FUCKING KILLING ME, RAX!"

Silence. From everybody. It was the first time any group of a hundred eleven-year-olds had ever been silent. A teacher had *screamed*. He had cussed, he had said *Jesus Christ,* and he'd said it about me.

What could I do? The bell rang, and I hit the locker room with the others, all of whom now avoided my eyes as if my humiliation were contagious. That afternoon, I forged a note from my mother excusing myself from Mr. Pyle's class for the remainder of the year, thanks to my "exercise-induced asthma." I couldn't have asked for a better outcome to my defeat, but it was still a resounding defeat.

The softball incident plumbed my deepest insecurities, sucking them up to the surface. What were those, exactly? That I was useless, destined to be a failure? In the locker room, fighting off tears, I considered that nothing I was good at was actually worth doing. I could read, but after age five so could everybody, and doing it too well in front of one's peers (or "showing off") earned one more scorn than anything else. I could write—same problem. Wait, maybe this was something: I had memorized one of Lenny Bruce's stand-up routines with what my dad said was astonishing speed. But he said that just before making me promise never to perform this particular talent for anybody else, especially not any of my gentile friends' parents, and so I didn't reckon it could be worth much either.

My skills may have earned me the placid approval of parents and English teachers, but I wanted a little of the hysterical worship that the sporty kids got. Even the people who disliked them (myself very much included) were impressed by them, for what they could do was bigger than school, bigger than themselves, even. Take Peter Jarvis. In class, I knew him as the psychopath who had evolved a shock of startling orange hair to warn would-be predators that he was poisonous. His hobbies included addressing his hijab-wearing classmates as "camel jockeys," carving threatening messages on the underside of my desk with the point of his compass . . . and basketball. He regularly led the chorus of complaints that I was "showing off" whenever

I read out loud in English class without making any mistakes, which he couldn't do. But no one showed off harder than him on the basketball court. Unlike mine, his talents were fun to see in action, and when he strutted them for us, we cheered.

Even I, watching Peter sail up to the hoop, could forget for a minute or two what he was like off the court. His gift swallowed up every character defect he had. My penchant for writing was different—it could only make me more of what I already was. If I was as useless as I feared, then I could only write my way into more uselessness. And no part of my body could transcend the problems of my mind or my character like Peter's could.

As I watched, I wondered where this otherwise unpleasant kid's grace and ability came from, in the same spirit that I might have wondered how a penniless acquaintance could afford to drive a BMW. There was no appreciable gap between what Peter wanted his body to do and what it could do, like there was with me. Was he giving himself commands: *dunk this ball, block this shot*? Or was he physically present in a way that I couldn't be, no more separate from his body's athleticism than he was from its blood and organs? I had never *been* my body like that. My brain was forever nudging it along, begging it to behave itself as it would have begged an unruly toddler.

"What are *you* looking at, psycho?" Peter asked rhetorically after yet another electrifying exhibition on the basketball court. He'd intended the question only to make me feel lousy, which it did—but it surprised me, too. What was *I* looking at? What *should* I look at, when here was this eleven-year-old kid, this hateful little shit, making shapes in midair that I hadn't even known existed, defying gravity, defying nature? I set my useless brain to the task of explaining this to him, but he jogged off the blacktop without waiting for an answer, presumably to carve more obscenities on my desk.

"Oh, that boy," my mother said later that day, dismissively knocking a knobble of ash off the tip of her cigarette. "He teases you because he likes you."

How could I explain it to her—that he teased me not because he liked me, but because he'd seen what I was, just as clearly as I had. I was a skilled reader and writer; Peter Jarvis was a god. Specifically the Greek kind of god, where you can partake of the divine while still being a huge asshole to people. We were establishing roles, all of us, and it was becoming more and more clear that mine would be to make impotent wisecracks about the world as I saw it. A god's role, naturally, was to put me in my place.

"Now sink your hips deeper . . . and raise your arms higher . . . and a bit deeper . . . and a little higher . . . and *hold!*"

The willowy woman leading my yoga class beams at all of us as we quiver and curse in our chair poses. My own personal hips are not sunk particularly deep, nor are my arms raised all that high, though I know I have the physical ability to correct my posture on both fronts. This half-assed performance is no longer something I give against my will, and I have no remaining desire to improve it. I suck at yoga purposefully and defiantly. *That'll teach you,* I think at the teacher, crackling with spite. Although, who am I really spiting? I'm the one paying to be here.

"Don't forget to breathe!" she calls out, and a chorus of

cranky inhales fills the room. It's a relief that the others don't like this much more than I do.

Some days I do try harder than this, but I take exception to this teacher's approach. She's smug. Giggly, too, and I can't think of a worse combination than those two qualities, especially when I encounter them in a fitness class. She giggles when she tells us to hold those damnable chair poses "only fifteen more seconds" just before making us do it for thirty, and then when we collapse afterwards, rubbing our legs, she giggles again. "I know," she says. "I'm soooo mean."

After my experience with Mr. Pyle all those years ago, I cannot, *will* not, be bossed around by a person with six-pack abs who sincerely wants me to do my best. Going to yoga at all is a huge deal for me, something I only began doing once merely sitting at my computer became too taxing for my poor neglected spine. At the conclusion of the six sessions that my insurance paid for, the physical therapist politely but firmly insisted that I was no longer allowed to spend all my leisure time sprawled out on the sofa waiting for death to come. Work out just *two hours* a week, he said with an unmistakable plea in his voice. So I'm here, because this is the only workout I could find that ends with a three-minute nap.

I did dabble in other strains of fitness for a while, cashing in the new-client specials of every gym and studio within a two-mile radius. This led, regrettably, to a sorry revival of my girlhood optimism that I was *just* about to discover the sport I was gifted at. Spin class was intolerable from the moment my teacher had to show me how to clip my shoes to my stationary bike—I knew that working out would begin humbly for me, but there's humble and there's being unable to put one's own shoes on without a tanned and grinning Australian man assuring one that one is "crushing it." Zumba might have been fun, but the nearest class to me took place in a children's karate studio, and it's hard to move with true aerobic abandon when there are twenty-five ten-year-olds earning their purple belts right next to you. And (rule of threes) Pure Barre was just plain creepy: teeny-tiny women performing teeny-tiny movements with their teeny-tiny thighs, while I panted thunderously next to them, quarantined by a foot-wide circle of sweat.

I hated admitting it, but it still hurt every time a form of fitness failed to take. The difference was that I now lived inside a shell of defense mechanisms that I'd built in the twenty years since Pylegate, fortified by John Hughes movies that cast jocks (or "sportoes," if you like) as the enemy. I would remember the Titans no longer, waste no more time on the lie that sports were central to a fulfilling life. If sports were central to anything, it was the life of the douchebag.

Take the Peter Jarvis of my yoga class, for example, whose name I don't know but have decided must be This Fucking Guy, since that's the only thing I ever call him in my head. I've never seen TFG wear a shirt, though he owns a vast array of joggers, shorts, and workout paraphernalia. While yoga offers the most fundamentally uncompetitive exercise regimen imaginable, he's figured out a way to imbue it with the same "FUCK YEAH, DUDE, GET SOME!" energy that plagues other workouts. I like to get to class early to ensure that I'll snag my favorite spot in the room—I'm very territorial about it. But one day I arrived and there he and his many abs were, a crew I'd never seen at this studio and didn't much like the look of. This Fucking Guy had set up in *my corner,* the better to practice his rather hideous, grunting headstands. After each one, he'd roll his body upright and look at the rest of us expectantly, maybe for applause.

Because TFG had stolen my corner, I had cosmic permission to detest him. Good thing, too, because I don't think he did one non-detestable thing the whole hour. When the teacher came in, he commanded her to spot him while he did more handstands or headstands, I forget which, some showy bullshit that the rest of us couldn't do. Class began, and his *ujjayi* breathing was, naturally, louder than everybody else's. Now I know you're thinking, *Rax, you beautiful fool, with that ass that just won't quit, how loud can a close-lipped "hhhhhhhh" really be?* And I'll thank you to watch your tone, but let me tell you: *Shockingly. Shockingly* loud. While the rest of us warmed up according to the teacher's instructions, he ignored her in favor of doing some other complicated, grunting inversion—in fact, I'm certain he spent more of that hour upside down than right side up. At the end, his *Om* rang out first and longest.

Like Peter Jarvis before him, This Fucking Guy could determine the most physically extreme version of any task and then just . . . do it, without preparing or even thinking about it that much. That was simply the way he operated. I hated him like I'd hated Peter—hell, it might've been the same lump of hate, dusty but still usable. He could do what I couldn't, what I had to struggle at, day after day, chipping away at my incapacity so slowly that I couldn't imagine the sculpture that would result, while he *was* the sculpture. He seemed like he always had been, like he was born in a headstand.

At this point, I hadn't seen Kommandant Pyle or Peter Jarvis in twenty years and could no longer reasonably blame them for my problems. But they did infect me with one germ that had proven tough to eradicate: the idea that my level of athletic skill *mattered*. It wasn't enough to swing the bat—I needed to either hit the ball or hate myself. In going to yoga at all, I'm swinging the bat, regardless of how much time I spend upside down, which is admittedly none. Still, that should satisfy me whether I hit the proverbial ball or not, being more than I've been willing to do for two decades. But I can always find some Peter Jarvis, some fucking guy, whose ease and command over his body make me wish I could erase mine off the face of the earth. If athletic skill matters, I don't. This is a wholly unrewarding thought exercise, one I can't seem to stop doing no matter how hard I try to Om my way to serenity.

I still think of myself as a paragon of sloth because that's the outfit I've put on just about every morning since I was born, but in reality, I go to yoga *four times* a week. I didn't believe that number could be correct when I counted it just now—maybe the past few weeks were unusually active? Maybe my apartment was being fumigated and I needed to find somewhere to be? No, I've been on a heavy yoga kick for months, railing against my slothful tendencies the whole time. I cuss and grumble when an instructor coaches me to wrangle my body into an especially taxing pose, but I do wrangle it.

It's occurred to me more than once that, in an apocalypse

scenario, I would be most useful as meat. But who cares about being useful? This Fucking Guy is covered in a thick shield of useful muscle, and he's also obnoxious. That's not what I drag my carcass to yoga for. Lately, I try to keep my eyes on my own test, so to speak—to avoid as best I can the dramatic comparisons between myself and the Peter Jarvises of the world. Part of the reason for this noble avoidance is that I just looked Peter up in the hopes of making a triumphant point about how I am, in fact, conclusively better than him only to learn that he's now a corporate lawyer with all kinds of high-profile clients and a wife who looks like a Disney princess. But mostly those comparisons require me to continue investing way too much attention in the notion of the body. I'm a writer, and as long as I can sit in a chair typing without having to go to the doctor about it, my body is perfectly fine. I don't have to be a basketball prodigy; I don't even have to be the best yoga-doer in the room. It's enough to be in the room at all, sweating and half-assing, yes, but in there just the same.

Some Notes Towards a Theory of an Old Dad

I learn early that I have an old dad.

My father is forty-seven when I'm born, which isn't *old*-old but it's old enough, especially in 1991. Older parents have become more of a norm, but thirty years ago, a man who hadn't had kids by forty-seven probably wasn't planning on having them at all. Later, when I'm an adult and my father begins telling me the things he's judged me to be old enough to hear, he admits that joy was not the couple's first reaction upon learning my mother was pregnant. The joy was there, he swears it, but it was buried, briefly, in other feelings—inadequacy, for example, and fear.

I don't notice my father's age right when I'm born, of course. Presumably, I'm occupied with more important things for a while, watching *Barney*, learning to read, but I do figure it out eventually—say around my seventh birthday. He's fifty-five then, and if forty-seven isn't *old*-old to raise a little kid, fifty-five sort of is. At least my father's brand of fifty-five. Age alone, numbers alone, can't account for the oldness of my dad. He's an old dad in spirit first, and then, too, in body. He will be old for the rest of his life.

Maybe I wouldn't have noticed for a while yet, only my friends' dads are all young and sporty. They're still protective of their dwindling youth; my dad's youth, snuffed out long before I was born, isn't something he even thinks about anymore except in wistful remembrances. At the pool, these muscular dads swim speedy laps for what feels like hours and hours. They wear sweat suits only to work out. To relax, jeans or khakis. They cook dinner some nights, consulting cookbooks with titles like *Healthy* and *Low-Carb* and *No-Guilt,* wearing aprons that promote the kissability of the cook.

At the pool, my father holds the wall and kicks his legs. This is called "Daddy's exercise," and, because I can do it faster than him, I disdain it. I'm young, with an unsubtle sense of what's good in the world; to me, everything worth doing is about strongest, fastest, best. Three things my old dad is not. I know from visiting my friends that real exercise involves a machine and a sweat suit. Also, sweat. He doesn't know or care, wears his sweat suit all the time irrespective of sweat.

My friends' dads all seem to be on, I don't know, middle-class sabbatical. They must work, some of them, only they're never *at* work when I come over. What a marvel, to see one's father in the daylight! Instead of working, these fathers are supervising the Tuscanization of their kitchens. They're heading out for a twenty-mile bike ride; they're making a watercress sandwich. They aren't watching TV, certainly not six hours' worth. They even play with us, and boisterously, their play muscles never having had childless decades during which to atrophy.

Somewhere in my unconscious, an association is forming. Other dads are young and hale. My dad is old and sick.

———————

I've inherited any number of irksome qualities from my father, but my least favorite by far is his old dadfulness. Despite being a young woman, I, too, am an old dad. They're everywhere once you know to look for them, these old dad types. Look for the serious-faced seventh grader popping Advil for his headache, or the ninety-two-year-old who's spent five decades assuming she's about to die despite not having anything actually wrong with her. This unfortunate condition is often comorbid with a Jewish background, though it's common in New Yorkers of any ethnicity, too, and artists. As a Jewish writer living in New York, I never had a chance. That's one of the symptoms, too: believing that one never had a chance.

Old dadfulness is easy to mistake for hypochondria, but it's more and less than that. A hypochondriac *worries* about being sick; an old dad doesn't have the energy. Hypochondria gives an anxious person a mission—to worry, to seek care—that no self-respecting old dad would ever accept. Many of us really do have some sort of chronic illness, however mild its expression may be, like my Crohn's disease, which can't be cured and intermittently wastes away my body when it flares up. The illness or lack thereof is beside the point. Even when my illness is in remission, I slog through life unwell, gloomy as an Eeyore. I may be healthy today, but tomorrow I will surely get sick, and in any event the world itself is a sick place, so why bother sprucing up my corner of it? That's our credo, thanks to which we're prone to alcoholism and a rather doleful strain of ADHD.

We complain. Have you noticed? We try to be funny when we do it, at least.

An old dad's work is never done. You can tell because his desk is covered, constantly, in all the work he hasn't done.

Old dadfulness is fear, calcified by despair.

When my friends and I would play tag as kids, I developed the technique of refusing to outrun whoever was It. They'd tag me, and I would be It, which was like being king of the playground. I could saunter anywhere I pleased and everyone else would clear out of my way; I set the pace, and no one could touch me. Being at the mercy of It, running when It ran, this sounded like anxious work to me. Giving up early was the closest I ever came to having fun while playing tag.

You hear that? The self-pity, the resignation? Old dad logic, through and through.

Alex Portnoy was an old dad. No other type of person would waste his one opportunity to narrate a great novel on a book-length psychoanalysis session. Humbert Humbert was an evil old dad, and Pa Karamazov, too—it's easier to find examples of evil old dads in literature than it is to find neutral or even decent ones, I assume because the evil is the only thing that makes all that whining passivity fun to write or exciting to read.

Lenù is an old dad; Lila is not. Obviously, Toad is ten times the old dad that Frog, that sniveling optimist, could ever be. You might assume that Cormac McCarthy's various grim protagonists are old dads, but I say no—you don't see a lot of us who are *grizzled*. We're a soft people.

Thanks to Jean Rhys (herself an incurable old dad until the day she died) and her novel *Wide Sargasso Sea,* I consider Bertha from *Jane Eyre* to be a literary old dad. Jane herself doesn't make the list, being plucky.

It has been suggested to me that Keith Richards is an old dad. This is, to my mind, a lazy interpretation of the lifestyle. Merely doing a shitload of heroin doesn't make someone a member of the tribe! I get why people fail to see this, since heroin's sort of a sad-sack drug, but Keith Richards has always seemed pretty cheerful to me.

Of all the Spice Girls, Sporty strikes me as the most likely to be one of us. Posh, too, clearly has the germ in her, though I believe that her staggering wealth and her marriage to David Beckham have inoculated her against the harshest effects of it.

Reclusiveness being an old dad's trait, Eve Babitz was one, at least in the back half of her life. Nora Ephron was not, ever. Joan Didion could be one, but more typically reeled in the whining before it hit old dad levels, or else cooled it by reporting on the facts. Reporting on the facts is anathema to most of us, as it requires us to set aside our mewling, complaining miasma and look at reality.

That said, Joan Didion did suffer, as I do, from migraines—the old dadliest of disorders. A migraine is invisible, stemming from no bleeding wound, no tumor. The illness all but forces its sufferers to be defensive about their pain. What could be more old dad than that?

The Western canon, by the way, is lousy with old dads, particularly the German philosophers. It seems that philosophy (and being German, too, for that matter) is the rare pursuit for which our tendencies towards gloom and obsession are advantageous.

Somewhat surprisingly, an old dad makes a great friend. All the time we spend stewing in our worthlessness makes us sympathetic listeners when you're down. If you get sick, there we'll be, carrying a quart of the same soup we chug every time we wrongly suspect we're getting sick. We give excellent advice, too, and spend generously on our friends. An old dad sets a lot of store by what he can do for the Good Samaritans who have agreed to be his friends. My father inherited ten thousand dollars from his stepfather's untimely death, and he immediately gave it all to a friend. This was no act of altruism. He bought for ten thousand dollars what he could have gotten for free: the right to stay in his friend's life.

I love my friends this much, too. I love them so much that I stay away from them most of the time, to spare them the burden of my company. I hope my friends are like bees: if I don't move, if they don't see me, they'll forget they hate me. They don't, of course, but nobody ever hated anybody as much as my closest friends hate me in my head.

I occupy a grandparently role in my friendships: I send money when they need it, text them on their birthdays, and spend a lot of time wishing they would call.

People are often surprised to hear me describe myself as shy. In person, I'm chatty and buzzy, even jittery. My eyes dart around like a lizard's. I bob my leg if I'm sitting, and arrange and rearrange my arms ceaselessly if I'm standing. (This is not a rhetorical question: How do human beings hold their arms? Please email raxkingisdead@gmail.com with answers.)

Parties, now that I can no longer drink and snort my way into an approximation of ease, are painful. I introduce different sets of friends to each other with the gusto most people reserve for setting up an orgy. I want them to love each other because of me, so that even if I rarely see them, they will have no choice but to think of me when they're together.

Then, realizing how much I've been vamping all night, I flee. Old dads are masters of the Irish goodbye. We aren't too drunk to make a more graceful exit, understand. Just too ashamed.

I began exhibiting symptoms of old dadfulness at the tender age of three. I was so afraid of everything that my parents thought I had become, to use the clinical term, a giant pussy. At that age, I feared dogs, adults, loud noises, the dark, needles, adults laughing loudly (distinct from both "adults" and "loud noises") . . . I could, but won't, go on. Any three-year-old might be afraid of any one of those things, of course. The problem was that I was terrified of them all, and at a high enough level that I'd become withdrawn and closed off.

You may not have noticed it recently, but the world outside your home is filled to bursting with dogs, adults, loud noises, the dark, and, depending on the character of your neighborhood, needles. In practice, I was afraid all the time. My parents thought I'd better see a psychiatrist about it, and so I began a short-lived series of visits with my father's analyst, Dr. Hyde.

In my memory, Dr. Hyde was ten feet tall and one hundred

years old, which probably puts him at about five-nine and sixty. He was a silvery sort of person: silver beard, silver rings, mellifluous silver voice. He was an adult, but then, most psychiatrists are adults—for this one fear, I felt I had been adequately prepared. What I didn't know to expect was that Dr. Hyde worked out of his beautiful Georgetown home, which he shared with (please, God, no) a big smelly dog.

I mean, forget it. He might as well have been a pile of needles cackling in the dark. When my knock at the door elicited a massive *woof,* I glared at my father accusingly. "You didn't tell me there was a *dog,*" I said.

"Baby, I'm sorry," he said, automatically hoisting me up on his shoulders so I wouldn't have to come face-to-face with the beast. Through my fear, I registered the rare pleasure of being picked up, something my father was often too exhausted to do. The only thing capable of besting his old dad tendencies was his desire to protect me from mine.

"I am *not,*" I said imperiously from my throne, "going somewhere with a *dog.*"

"I'm afraid you have to see Dr. Hyde, but maybe he can lock up the dog," he said. "Maybe he can even help you not be afraid of dogs anymore."

This was a horrifying new possibility. Not be afraid of dogs? But then how would I avoid getting bitten by one? This twisted system of inputs and outputs was how I saw the whole world: I could control my input of unpleasant experiences with a consistent output of fear and vigilance. The fear kept me realistic, and the vigilance kept me safe.

———————

It might sound like an old dad is immune to joy, but in fact when his brain springs into delight, it does so completely. No one takes lustier advantage of a sunny day in May than an old dad; no one houses a burger with greater gusto. What makes his cell-level misery intolerable is that he knows, always, what he's missing. He's locked inside an electrified fence. He can peer through it at the beautiful terrain on the other side, he can frolic there for a few hours at a time, but he will never be permitted to live there.

Perversely, old dad types tend to be attractive. I don't mean they're pretty or handsome—some are, some aren't—but they reliably exert an attracting force on potential lovers. The self-loathing that twists up their insides like a babka presents, at first, as an appealing thoughtfulness and sensitivity. They can make you feel like you're the only person who understands them, because they're worried that you will be.

Still, they're mysterious and glamorous—at first. But mystery and glamour are two qualities that evaporate once you fall in love with a person, and it's then that the fundamental claustrophobia of a relationship with an old dad asserts itself. Your air smells like him, every last gulp of it. You eat what he likes to eat. Once, you felt honored and important: you were the only person who understood him. Now you feel trapped: you are the only person who understands him.

I spent months recently dealing with random stabbing pains in the bottom of my right foot while walking around in the beat-up Doc Martens I wore every day. The pains were so unpredictable and so severe that I became a timid walker, taking each step like I owed it money. I'd pull off my boots at the end of the day and observe what appeared to be a stigmata on the bottom of the offending foot. Sometimes the hole was caked in dried blood, other times it was only raw. Always it was pain-colored, the same velvety scarlet that now stained the boot's lining.

This went on, as I said, for months, and I never thought to check the bottom of my boot. Why would I? I lived in constant expectation that this would happen—maybe not *this*, but some inexplicable agony that would torture me psychologically and make me bleed. If anything, the blood was satisfying to see. So many of my problems, as my loved ones were wont to remind me, were all in my head. I wanted to show my foot wound to those same loved ones: *See? They're not* all *in my head.*

Then, one day, I stepped a bad step in front of my friend Mike and cried out, as usual. Rather than drop everything to envelop me in concern, Mike asked, "Something in your shoe?"

"No," I said. "That just happens sometimes. I don't know what it is."

"You sure? Lemme see."

God, I was so confident as I handed over my boot. *Just you wait*, I thought with relish. I tried to give him a peek at my bleeding foot wound for effect, but he was looking at the boot, not me. After a moment, he burst out laughing.

"Oh, *Rax*," he said. And he handed me a bent, rust-colored nail about an inch long.

The illusion of my mysterious foot stigmata, in which I'd lived so comfortably over the past several months, fell away in an instant. Rather than feel relief at identifying and solving a problem, I immediately missed the unsolvable problem I'd thought I had. There was nothing grand or significant about what I'd been going through all this time. Only a rusty nail.

"Come on, buddy," he said, handing my boot back sans nail. "Let's go get you a tetanus shot." And away we went, passing any number of dogs and laughing adults on the way to urgent care. There was a lesson to be learned from that rusty nail, but I already knew I wouldn't learn it.

Dr. Hyde never fixed my old dadfulness because, from his perspective, there was nothing to fix. He told my parents I was perfectly fine, and the message I received from the whole experience was to stop telling them what I was afraid of. It's not the good doctor's fault that "old dad" does not appear in any edition of the DSM. This was a condition I had to diagnose on my own, and I've decided it's incurable. If it *is* curable—if I'm not obligated by nature to spend my life suspended in stale windless air—then I'll eventually have to square with the reality that I could have cured it, and didn't.

Hey Big Spender

"We're celebrating, baby," my father said to me, opening his arms for a hug. "Dinner's on me, anywhere you and your mother want to go. In fact, dinner's on me all weekend!"

My father had just won a case, and grandly rejected my suggestion that we celebrate with Happy Meals (I had my eye on a *Mulan* toy). He explained that you might celebrate with a Happy Meal if you'd found a wadded-up twenty in the street, but he'd made *real* money on this case, *serious* money, the Palm money. I was unimpressed by the idea of steaks at the Palm. What small child gets fired up to eat a massive piece of meat that hasn't even been thoughtfully molded into nugget form and deep-fried? But when I learned that I would be permitted—nay, encouraged—to wear a frilly dress, I softened.

We went to the Palm, where I was enchanted by the sight of a white-clad waiter pushing a dessert cart around the restaurant. The bartenders were brewing a range of fascinating potions, coupes spilling over with deep orange, a chilled martini glass hissing at the first dribble of gin. Every woman was dressed like a princess from one of my storybooks. Most enchanting of all,

I seemed to be the only kid in the place. We were a long way from McDonald's, that was for sure.

At our table, my initial sense of wonder quickly faded to boredom. This was not a place where I could use the restaurant's crayons to draw on the tablecloth, which was actually made of cloth, not just paper for me to doodle on like the one at Luigi's Pizza. I saw now why I was the only kid in the room: there was nothing for a kid to do, and I was the only one fool enough to waste my time here. Worst of all, there was no children's menu, meaning no hope of chicken nuggets.

But my father was happy. Lord, was he happy! Even my mother allowed herself to be swept up in the mood of the Palm, the magic of its dark wood and golden light. That night, my parents exuded ease in a way that they'd never done before. They joked with each other and with me. My father sweet-talked our waiter into tracking down some buttered noodles and printer paper for me to eat and doodle on, respectively. My mother, in a burst of whimsy, took me to the bathroom to "freshen up," painting her usually forbidden lipstick all over my mouth. And it was all thanks to my father's victory at work—meaning, it was all thanks to money.

Money, I already knew, was a trickster. There seemed to be no way to pin him down, convince him to stay for the long haul. He was either there or he wasn't, based on wherever his whims led him. Whether we had or had-not, my father worked from early morning till late, sometimes deep into the night, and how hard he worked had no recognizable relationship to money's presence in our house. Even as I gobbled up my noodles, I sensed that tonight's celebratory dinner might easily turn into tomorrow's "Who here owns stock in the electric company?" All my father knew how to do with money when it showed up was enjoy it thoroughly—it wasn't like it was going to stick around. The idea was to beat the money to the punch, to spend it on things you liked before it could get garnished by a debt collector or sucked up into an interest payment.

When I turned eighteen, my father told me that the government was going to pay me five thousand dollars.

"Wow!" I said, overdrawn-bank-accountishly. "What's the occasion?"

"Because I hit retirement age before you turned eighteen," he said. "It's from Social Security."

"But you're not retired."

"You don't want the money? Fine, I'll keep the money," he said. "I'll buy myself a boat. And name it *Daddy's Retirement*."

Well, I just couldn't let that happen. For one thing, I did want the money. Then, of course, I didn't want to be responsible in any way for the existence of a boat named *Daddy's Retirement*. Shortly thereafter, I received a check from Social Security, and shortly after that thereafter, all five thousand of the dollars were spent. It took me one summer.

Where did the money go? Some to rent, some to bills, some to drugs, some to the municipal economy of San Francisco— I'd never visited the West Coast and, emboldened by my newly fattened-up bank account, flew out there on a whim to see what I could see. But even that trip wasn't as extravagant as it might sound, since I bought the cheapest airline tickets I could find and slept on a stranger's couch instead of splurging on a hotel.

Most of the money went where most of my money always goes: nowhere. I went nowhere interesting, I bought nothing noteworthy, and yet at the end of that summer the money was, inarguably, gone.

"Oh, my God," my father groaned when I sheepishly answered his question about how I was making out with my big Social Security payday. "Oh, my *God*. You're just like me."

Years before, whenever my parents had their hushed conversations about our finances, the money had seemed like a whole third person in the conversation—one who was on my father's side, supporting his case and shutting down my mother's. She had many questions about his spending, but he always had an answer, or at least such an obstreperous argument that she quickly gave up the fight. When they filed their taxes, my father had her fill out her paperwork first and then completed his in absolute secrecy, even covering pages with his hand if she walked in the room. Of course, I hadn't noticed this as a girl, taxes being the absolute stupidest of stupid grown-up goings-on. All I ever noticed back then was that my father was fun with money while my mother was boring.

My mother doesn't see the amount of money in her bank account as a challenge: *How quickly can I make this disappear?* She's a careful spender who is, to this day, saving up for retirement, despite the fact that she retired five years ago. Her cautiousness is admirable—it's hard to argue against the virtue of treating money with care—but, in its way, it's just as anxious as my father's spending was. My father couldn't have money without looking for ways to burn it, while my mother can't have money without worrying about how it will be taken from her.

Either way, it seems, the point of the money isn't in the having but rather in the imagining of how it will disappear. Some people are invigorated by this imagining, and others are frightened.

Recently, I invited my mom to come stay with me for a few days. "Come on—don't you want to check out Sean's and my new place?"

"Well," she said slowly, and I wanted to ask her to just stop talking, because I knew what was coming. "I just don't think now is a good time. I mean, New York is so expensive."

"Yeah, but your only expense would be getting here," I pointed out. "The train is like thirty dollars. You can stay here for free. We can cook all our meals."

We proceeded in this unsatisfying fashion, all the more unsatisfying because I could hear the pain in her voice, how much she wanted to come visit and how she genuinely did not believe it was possible. The numbers said it was, but her spirit told her otherwise. My dad, on the other hand, would have blown his last dollar on flying here first-class and insisted on putting us both up in the fanciest hotel he could book on his maxed-out credit card. I don't want to go completely broke every single year, and I also don't want to spend a week eating eggs for dinner as penance every time I dare to treat myself to a haircut, so it seems that both my parents' approaches are wrong. But unfortunately for my mother, only my father's is *glamorously* wrong, so it rules the day.

Every now and then, a cable news program will strap a mic to some dipshit with an economics degree whose job is to tell us young people that we're spending too much money on nonsense. Well, he never says "nonsense"—whenever this guy appears to scold us, he's got a convincingly specific boogeyman in mind, some routine five-dollar purchase that we don't even realize is standing between us and homeownership. One year the boogeyman was avocado toast, another year it was pumpkin spice lattes. The object doesn't matter as much as the assertion that it is frivolous and our love for it is a big mistake.

The Economics Dipshit would have a heart attack if he could hear me explain my own personal money management policy, which is, in essence: spend all the money you have, all the time. The collections agency can't take it away from you if you've already converted it into toys. Sure, they'll start garnishing your wages at some point, but we'll all be dead by then, probably. It's the perfect crime!

What the Dipshit never seems to understand is that we all come by our money neuroses honestly. The agony of handling money is just one more thing passed down through the generations epigenetically. My father, despite being the problem parent in this regard, never encouraged my profligacy. Indeed, seeing it in action caused him real and obvious guilt. He told me all the right things about avoiding instant gratification and being a shrewd saver, but he told me never to take up cigarette smoking, too, and yet every day I watched him suck down cigarettes like they were his multivitamins, watched him order hundreds of dollars' worth of Hammacher Schlemmer paraphernalia that he never even unwrapped once it arrived, watched him live the exact luxuriously appointed life he was coaching me to avoid. "Yes, but your father has the most rotten credit of any man alive," my mother warned me, but all I heard was: *Your father has taste, and style.*

I eventually learned that my dad had been raised by a luxury pig, too—his stepfather, Hiram. My paternal grandfather died before my father was born while training to fly fighter planes in WW2, and my dad spent the first several years of his life cooped up with a penniless teenage mother: thence his desire for the finer things. Then, when he was still a boy, his mother remarried a shadowy Boston lawyer who showered them both with expensive toys: thence the finer things themselves.

"I don't know. His business was his business," my bubbe would say of her second husband, often apropos of nothing. "How should I know what all he was up to? You want I should ask him? Here—" and she'd take her Ouija board down from the shelf where it lived with her tarot cards and instruments for astrological divination. "Here. You ask him. I'm busy."

It's true enough that she never knew everything her husband was up to. He hid his financial affairs from his family the same way my father would hide his years later, developing an air of thrilling mystery that his kids tried to decode. Because he told them nothing, they had to trade out-of-context tidbits among themselves as if they were his fan club: On this day, Hiram came home from work at two in the morning, whispering with two hulking "associates." The next day, he took the family on a spontaneous trip to New York, staying in the finest hotels and lavishing them all with costly souvenirs; and three days later, for reasons known only to him, the family was penniless again. The kids found him fascinating, but they were also trying to figure out why their lives were so chronically unstable, rapid-cycling between opulence and penury for years. My bubbe had three mink coats, but the house's electricity was cut.

Then, one day, Hiram moved the family of five to Miami in the middle of the night. He never told them why this move had to happen at two in the morning, and according to my father, nobody asked; it must have seemed like one of those questions, more and more frequent in that family, that would only be answered with a weighty silence and a stormy mood. In Miami, they lived in a two-bedroom apartment: three teenage kids crammed into a single room. But the rules in Florida were different than in Boston, with its stifling New England WASP social codes. Here, it was okay to be a striving Jew with a tackily dressed wife; it was expected.

The family threw itself enthusiastically into the possibilities offered by being good-time Jews in 1960s Miami, and the city seems to have embraced them warmly—for a time. There's an article in the *Miami Herald* about their tiny apartment, into which my bubbe had gamely crammed the ornate furniture and pottery that Hiram had bought her during various flush periods, the stuff she hadn't been forced to sell off. "It's a little bit of Boston on the bay," she says, sounding very *Better Homes & Gardens*. A couple other blurbs dot the *Herald*'s society pages about what the glitzy couple wore to the theater one night, or whose party they were seen attending. The next article that shows up is an interview with one of Hiram's former colleagues regarding their business together. It's headlined "I Was Threatened by the Mafia!"

Well!

It seems that Hiram had been trying to break into organized crime for years, always via petty schemes that brought luxury into the house for weeks at a time before his payout was drained. The biggest scheme he ever managed seems to have entailed holding stock in his and his friends' names for some mobster who was not legally permitted to own it himself. If Hiram had saved any of his money, ever, one such petty scheme would've been enough to take care of the family for years. But like my father, he seems to have been allergic to the quiet comfort of paying bills and saving sensibly. How can such middle-of-the-road living—such *gutless* living—compete with the thrill of leading one's impoverished family to the driveway one morning to scream and gasp over their brand-new Cadillac?

What was the extent of Hiram's involvement in organized crime? Like my bubbe said, how should I know? Everyone who did know is long dead, including Hiram himself, who was killed in an airplane fire while flying back to Miami from the Bahamas with some of his "associates" in 1969. On top of that, he was impossible to question, being a lawyer with a nasty temper. He could out-cross-examine anyone who wanted to know what was up with his finances, and on the off chance that failed, there was always the timeless negotiation tactic that's been passed down in my family for generations, "rear up in a frightening rage." Long after he died, the people who had known him stayed tight-lipped about his work and his money.

I do know, though, that my father's approach to financial planning had its roots in Hiram's. First, you amass as much income as you possibly can, working so much your loved ones rarely see you. Then you blow it all to smithereens, on toys and trinkets, cars and parties, lest "the bastards" have a chance to take it from you.

———

When I was growing up, my family usually had plenty of cash. Or, at least, my father had plenty of cash, until the terrible recurring moment when he'd spent it all, before which moment a bit of the cash trickled down to my mother and me. After he'd bought luxury cars, visited opulent New York hotels, and treated his friends to extravagant outings, we were next on his list. She and I were destined to be left out of his money benders—unlike my complacent bubbe, my mother couldn't be relied on to keep her mouth shut and leave the money matters to him. He liked taking her out and showing her off, but if she'd been welcomed into this lifestyle fully, she would have figured out just how much he was spending and the party would've been over. Instead, he brought us souvenirs from his other life. Jewelry for her, state-of-the-art toys for me. It was as if he'd emigrated to a land of opportunity, coming home periodically to shower gifts on the family he'd left behind.

He wasn't being intentionally mean or stingy, leaving us in the cold like that. He just couldn't stand to lose this fantasy world that he'd just barely managed to buy into, and there was no place for a prudent wife or a needy daughter there. The unspoken reason for his spending, setting aside the fact that he would have been bad with money no matter the circumstances, was that most of his friends were filthy rich. We had cash, vulgar and prone to running out; they had *assets*. How else could he maintain the illusion that he was keeping up with them? Their friendship was a poker table, and the minimum bet was high.

Plus—and this part I can speak to from firsthand experience—nothing in the world is more fun than wasting money. The more frivolous the expense, the better; the more precarious your situation after spending it, the better. I'm no adrenaline junkie, except when it comes to my bank account. Imagine you're booking a hotel. If you book the cheapest one you can find without asking questions, congratulations, you and my husband have a lot in common. But if you're like me, you casually scroll past the places whose names include "Econo," into the listings that cost two hundred dollars a night. Except, well, two hundred a night is already too expensive—why, with fees it's practically three hundred! So you might as well upgrade your visit again, and then, why not?, one more time, until finally you've added to your virtual cart some exotic thing called an executive suite with a jacuzzi and butler service.

You hardly even realize you've done it, is the thing. Jacuzzis gross you out and the idea of having a literal butler makes you nervous—what if that guy *bows* at you? But it's hard to argue with your joyriding heartbeat, with your imaginings: your worn old soles skidding down a marble lobby, the sweet stink of wealth in the air. Before you click that PURCHASE button, you try, half-heartedly, to talk yourself out of it. But by now, several upgrades into this reservation, there's no turning back. The desire to blow a thousand dollars is a rope pulling taut inside you. You press that button. The rope snaps. Orgasm, afterglow: the thing is bought, and now that you can't go back, you might as well adore it. That feeling, more than any specific purchase, is what I'm chasing—the weightlessness of irresponsibility, before the consequences set in.

There was a time when the game was relatively stress-free, when I believed my father could have thrown me a bone in a true emergency. I was wrong, but like Hiram before him, he was skilled at hiding the direness of his situation from me. All that changed when he got sick, losing the ability he'd always had to replenish his supply of cash by working more. By the time I entered college, he'd spent nearly every dollar he was ever going to make, and he still had a decade left to survive somehow. The party was finally over—for him.

For me, it was just beginning. My false sense of security yanked out from under me, I could play for real stakes, I could test my own ability to regenerate cash the way he'd always managed to do at the last second, just before serious trouble descended on him. It wasn't compulsive spending, what we were doing. This was real-life alchemy, and so what if it came with a little risk? Having a full, exciting life meant accepting risk! It's the exact thing that goes through a compulsive gambler's head as he recklessly bets the family house, but I told myself that my behavior didn't count as gambling. Gamblers *wasted* money; I converted it into good cheer, in the form of clothes I didn't need and drugs that were, often as not, bunk.

The Economics Dipshit is wrong to assert that, if only I hadn't treated myself to that plate of spaghetti in San Francisco, I would be making my first mortgage payment now. Life's big purchases—cars, homes, *Daddy's Retirement*—these were always going to be beyond my means. And because I've never expected them, I haven't longed for them, any more than I've longed to be king of England or climb the world's most remote mountain. Even before the 2008 financial crisis, when my entire generation learned that it was never going to own jack shit, I sort of knew I'd never own a home. I'm just not the "mortgage type." All of which is to say, warnings from the Economics Dipshit have consistently failed to scare me straight. He claims I could turn my avocado toast money into a down payment, I see that I can't, and I ignore him.

Still, much as it pains me, I must admit that the Dipshit has a point. No, I couldn't buy a house with the money I spend on pointless treats. But looking at my bank statements, I see that I could buy *some*thing: a cavity filling, a pair of waterproof winter boots. Trouble is, these purchases are not, in any way, amusing. Who ever had fun paying down a maxed-out credit card? The joy is in *wasting* money, in blowing it on luxuries that are definitionally out of your reach rather than sensibly squirreling it away until you can afford new glasses.

Because I know this is bananas and I persist in believing it anyway, I've become just as secretive about money as Hiram and my father always were. My husband, Sean, is sensible and therefore boring. He loves to say things like "But we just went out to dinner last night" and "Didn't you already buy one bikini for this trip?" Ugh! Wretched stuff. So I treat us both to experiences regardless of whether I can afford them, and then I gallantly refuse to even tell him how much they cost: *Don't deny me the pleasure of treating you, baby!* My seeming generosity is, in fact, pure selfishness—if he knew how much this dinner cost, we'd have to go without extravagant treats for weeks. Of the two of us, only I have the crucial skill of spending far beyond my means without worrying my pretty little head about it.

"Don't worry your pretty little head about it," I say when he offers to pay for a spa treatment that I know neither of us can afford but that I am insisting we get anyway. "I got a discount."

I got a discount is the classic guilty lie of big spenders everywhere, and I'm just now realizing that it must have been a lie every time my father said it to me, too.

My father grew up with the understanding that money and secrecy are inherently entangled, and because he did, I did too. I suppose this is a common enough lesson—we all absorb variants on it, learning that it's rude to ask people how much things cost or how much they get paid. In those cases, though, the argument is mostly one of tact and sensitivity, at least on the surface: you don't want to make people *feel bad* about their finances, whether they're in better or worse shape than yours. With Hiram, you didn't worry about making him feel bad, but about putting yourself in danger. If he didn't answer your questions, he would frighten you into silence; on the rare occasion that he did, the answers themselves were dangerous. And while my father's work was on the up-and-up—there would never be any articles about *him* threatening anyone—he could be just as scary in the face of questioning about his financial behavior. Confronted with his reddening face and bugging eyes, the questions would stop, and the behavior need never change.

I don't want to be either shady or angry about money, and I'm not in a position where I necessarily have to be. My work is legal and it pays for everything I need. But like Hiram, I want to surprise my family with the Cadillac in the driveway. My reflex is still to distract and deflect every time money comes up in conversation with my husband, and there's not even that much to distract and deflect *about*. It feels awfully pathetic, arguing about the supposedly good and important reasons I bought a bespoke dog sweater.

Well, at least, it *would* feel pathetic arguing with Sean about the dog sweater, if we'd actually argued about it. But lately I've noticed that my ridiculous spending plays an important role in our marriage: it gives him permission. Sure, I wheedle him to let me reserve us a last-minute table at Le Twelve Course Tasting Menu—A Daniel Boulud Concept™ instead of cooking bean stew for dinner like we'd planned. Still, despite his insistence that he cares about tiresome nonsense like saving money, he doesn't take much wheedling. He'll complain that we've been eating out way too much lately, but once we're seated at our table, he's the one oohing and aahing over the exquisite service, wondering aloud whether we'll be able to live with ourselves if we don't order the optional chef's cheese course for an additional thirty dollars each.

"I don't know," I say, relishing this moment each time it comes. "We've been eating out way too much lately, no?"

"But we're already here," he says—and he's right, we are, we're here, because *I* was the one with the guts and gumption to demand that we come here. He saw an unnecessary expense and wanted to dodge it; I barreled us directly into it, howling a battle cry. I won, and now he's having the time of his life! I don't doubt that my mom had the time of hers, too, once in a while. Lots of relationships are made up of a profligate spender and a careful one, and the profligate spender gets a pretty bad rap, particularly when the relationship ends and everyone learns just how deep in debt they are. But what about all the fun that money paid for? Doesn't that count for anything?

You might think that, because I spend money like I'm about to die, I'm patient with the financial excesses of others. Far from it—I love pointing out other people's bad financial behavior, as long as they make more money than I do. It's cruel to shit on someone whose finances have already shit on them, and you'll never hear a peep out of me regarding the excesses of people buying lobsters with their SNAP benefits. But anyone with a nice high income who admits to struggling just isn't being *responsible* enough. Look out, people who earn six figures and still believe times are tight: I've convinced myself that yours is the specific salary that will fix me. It really is obnoxious when rich people complain about not having enough for a private jet, but that isn't the spirit in which I jeer at these big spenders. I'm not righteously concerned about any injustice or hypocrisy; I'm *jealous*. I could be so much worse with their money than they are. As far as I'm concerned, the problem isn't my attitude about spending, but the amount of money available for me to waste, as if I'm not capable of finding out-of-reach objects to covet at every price point. Go ahead, take away every dollar I have and send me to live in the swamp. Come back in six months, and I'll be in debt to an alligator.

"Oh, my *God*. You're just like me," my father said about my irresponsible treatment of the *Daddy's Retirement* Fund all those years ago, but he looked shifty and guilty as he said it. "Don't even think about hitting me up for a loan."

"What? I wasn't," I said, taken aback. "When have I ever hit you up for a loan?"

"Because you need to learn to be responsible with money. I mean it. I'm not giving you a cent. You'll have to get a job."

"Hello! I have *two* jobs," I said, watching his inexplicably guilty face as it tried to right itself into an expression of fatherly fury. "Why are you weird today? You're all . . . blinky."

"Blinky! Blinky! My girl, it's time you learned that a man has a *right*—"

"Holy shit." I j'accuse-pointed at the brand-new, 65-inch TV mounted on his wall. His chest, which had been working itself into a state of righteous puffiness, deflated. "Is that why you're not giving me a cent?"

"I would urge you not to make too much of this."

"You really need to learn to be responsible with money," I said. "Don't even think about hitting me up for a loan."

"Your situation and mine are absolutely not the same!"

"Yeah, I *traveled*," I said. "I *enriched* myself. You bought a giant box that makes you stupider to replace the perfectly good stupidity box you had before."

He couldn't argue with that, and so I sank back into the pillowy glory of a rare triumph over my father. We watched his new stupidity box in silence for a few minutes. I wondered how much it had cost, and realized a similar purchase was to blame for every other time he'd preemptively warned me not to even think about asking for a loan. No wonder he bellowed with rage every time it seemed like his financial behavior might come to light. Better to frighten your family than let them see you laid low by your own bad decisions.

"The picture is way clearer than on your last one," I admitted.

"Yeah," he said with gruff pleasure. "Worth the money."

Commitment Issues

Missing a train by ten seconds and waiting half an hour for the next one? *I'm gonna fucking kill myself.*

Asking the name of someone who has already told it to me several times and is offended that I don't remember meeting her? *I'm gonna fucking kill myself.*

Saying something I believe to be sharp and funny in the group chat, only for my remark to be met with silence followed by the rest of the chat politely moving on to a new topic? *I'm gonna fucking kill myself.*

Now, I'm sure I'm not the only person who's ever had that thought while e.g. watching a train's doors close from the wrong side of them, an experience designed to make even the sanest person yearn for the sweet silence of the void. But most of those people probably don't proceed to fantasize about it, hungrily, in detail. When I think *I want to die,* it's in the just-kidding-unless-you're-into-it tone of someone who wants to make a sexual advance but isn't willing to fully commit to it.

Wanting to die does not necessarily mean I'm unhappy. Does a spy swallow a cyanide pill rather than submit to questioning because he's unhappy? That's how I look at suicide: an unfortunate but plausible method of avoiding enemy capture. It's just that my enemies aren't the terrorists or the Nazis, but my own thoughts. They're relentless, they're always spying on me, and they'll only die when I do.

Fortunately, I have plenty of footage from my past to obsessively review, should the events of my daily life prove insufficiently ideation-worthy. You can't always wait for something horrible to happen when your brain decides it's time to have suicidal depression. While falling asleep, I might fire up the internal video labeled "Remember When You Asked Out That Guy on AIM and He Printed Out the Conversation and Taped Copies of It to Everyone's Locker?" That one gets me every time, but if I'm looking for a more somber strain of suicidality, there's always "Can You Believe You Kept Working for the Three Weeks When, in Retrospect, It Was Totally Obvious That Your Dad Was Dying?" In the years before I sought treatment for my troubled mind—in the years, too, when I pursued treatments that weren't working—I'm sure I looked pretty lethargic, sleeping till noon and staring slack-jawed at any professor who asked me a question. But my brain was the Lincoln Tunnel at five o'clock on a Friday.

I didn't think much about my cyanide-pill approach to emotional regulation until the physical I had during my sophomore year of college, during which the school nurse casually asked, "By the by, do you suffer from depression?"

"Most definitely," I said, and she looked alarmed for a moment before collecting herself.

"No, no, not like that." She chuckled at my obvious misunderstanding. "I mean it in the sense of . . . like, you're not losing interest in your usual hobbies, are you?"

"Oh, yeah," I said. "Big time."

"Feeling distant from friends? Trouble getting out of bed in the morning?"

"Check. Check." This was fun!

But when the nurse finally asked, with some trepidation, whether I believed I'd be better off dead, I hesitated. The answer was both yes and no, only . . . neither answer painted a detailed enough picture. Neither did any of the yeses or no's that had come before. There was *context* to all my answers to this questionnaire. I did not want to die 100 percent of the time, and I didn't want it for no reason. I could agree that my brain was probably at fault, but so was life.

I'd always assumed that whatever mental illness I had would be diagnosed via biopsy or sample, a strange color on a brain scan or platelets misbehaving in my blood. I could feel that something was wrong with me, and when the time came, I assumed a doctor would be able to point out exactly what it was. But there was nothing comfortingly scientific or medical about this diagnostic process. How could this questionnaire reveal anything important about me? I could have written these questions myself, as last-minute homework for a class that didn't interest me.

"Sometimes," I said. "Sometimes I think that."

"We'll call that ten out of ten," the nurse said.

Thus began many excruciating years of trying like hell to treat my sorry brain.

I tried to kill myself during my first marriage. He was cheating on me; that would do for impetus. I did a piss-poor job of it, though. It was Tylenol, and it wasn't enough.

In the ambulance, I studied the EMTs who'd responded to my husband's call. It was just us three in there, and with my terrified husband out of frame, the inherent drama of a suicide attempt began to recede. I felt sheepish. Antsy, too. Maybe these guys could be persuaded to give me a little something to take the edge off. (That was the state of my grasp on reality: I honestly believed the function of the EMTs who had been called to save my life was to distribute "a little something to take the edge off.")

"O's looking good so far this year," one EMT said to the other.

"Real good. Taking the kid to Camden Yards for his birthday. His first game."

"No shit. He's turning how old?"

"Seven," said the EMT, swerving us through a red light, which reminded me that this was, technically, an emergency. That *I* was an emergency, one I'd caused for no reason except— I cringed—my *unhappiness*. How bourgeois.

The doctors in the ER were less impressed with my suicide attempt than my poor husband had been. One of them all but rolled her eyes when I explained my method to her. *Hmph!* Next time, I'd try something less childish—hanging, say, or a scarier pill.

Next time? Shouldn't there be no next time? It was hard to decide. The urge to die was a black spot shifting around my field of vision, impossible to look at and impossible to blink away.

One minute I wanted to kill myself, the next I wanted to just go home, forget any of this had ever happened.

The doctor handed me a paper cup of tar. "Swallow this," she said.

I looked askance at the tar.

"It's activated charcoal. So you don't absorb any more of that Tylenol into your liver."

"Shouldn't I, I mean . . . isn't there like a stomach pump, or . . . ?"

"Wouldn't you know it, there *is*," she said sarcastically. "But since I'm the one who's been to medical school here, why don't we try doing what I say, and then talk about a pump later if we have to?" (By the way, I still don't know what this doctor's fucking damage was. Sure, I was The Boy Who Cried I'm Going to Kill Myself, but don't big old phonies deserve a little bedside manner, too?)

I drank the tar. It tasted how it looked. I began dedicating my next suicide note to this very doctor, grandly forgiving her for being such an asshole. I'd already written one suicide note that day; I guess I had the bug. She had left the room but popped back in to remark that I was *so kind* to humor her by drinking the charcoal, her tone unmistakably that of a person who'd only thought of her brilliant rejoinder after ending the conversation. I revised the note in my head—less forgiving now.

A bed was found for me at a facility that my father assured me was "really nice," as if he were planning a resort vacation for me rather than a week in a mental hospital. "They have all sorts of cool stuff," he said brightly. "Games and, you know, food."

"I'm glad you managed to find a place that has food," I said.

My father didn't bat my nasty comment back at me, only pretended to laugh at it through the tears on his face, which told me things were bad. I felt numb and bloated. I shouldn't have tried to kill myself. I didn't have the courage to do it right, and now it was just one more fucking problem to solve.

At the Place, I yawned and fidgeted my way through intake. It was 2:30 A.M., and I asked the intake staff member whether we might be able to finish in the morning so I could get some sleep. The tone of her response heavily implied that I should have thought about that before I tried to kill myself.

Finally, she led me to my room, which had no lock and no doorknob—and, I soon learned, no darkness. Every half hour, a nurse opened the door, flooding the room with light while she made sure I wasn't dead. Then she'd leave, and I'd try to conk out before she came back, chronically suspended in the last heavy limbo before sleep.

Around four, I felt a rumble in my guts and went to the toilet, and there it was: the tar. Tight as a fist, black as pitch. A souvenir. With great relief, I flushed it away.

I met my fellow patients for the first time at breakfast, which at the Place was mandatory and at 6:30 A.M. I thought longingly of my lazy sleepings-in at home as I scanned the tables for somewhere to sit. One girl saw me looking and blocked the spot next to her with her tray. How was it possible that even here, there were cool kids?

That's when I realized something distressing: because the Place treated both drug addictions and mental disorders, its patients were tacitly divided into groups of Junkies and Crazies. I examined my cohort through sticky day-old contact lenses.

The Junkies were better-looking—they weren't being prescribed antipsychotics that made them break out and bloat.
They sucked and sucked at their nicotine inhalers, which didn't
look quite as cool as cigarettes, but in this context we all had to
take what we could get. I mimicked their bored facial expres-
sions, hoping they'd adopt me.

A nurse tapped my shoulder. "Blood," she said.

"Blood," I agreed.

"Gotta take your blood now," she said. "Before you eat any
breakfast."

Fair enough, but did she have to do it right there? The Junkies
watched from their table with disgust as the nurse siphoned my
blood, telling me an unsettling number of times that with God's
help the Place was going to make me better. It was mortifying,
like when your mom licks her finger and rubs dirt off your face
in front of your friends. Was it maybe, on some level, a relief
that I could still feel embarrassed by stuff like this—could it be a
sign that my brain was ready to give up its prima donna act and
get back to the business of everyday life? No, it was just embarrassing, on top of every other damn thing.

I made no headway with the Junkies that morning. But at
lunch, I managed to become fast friends, as I've done in every
setting for my entire adult life, with a heavily tattooed gay guy.
Kieran straddled the border of Junkie and Crazy just like I did,
was determined to make the Place slide off his back like I was.
He collapsed onto the empty bench next to me with a dramatic
sigh, rescuing me from a second meal alone.

"You're staring at my hair," he said by way of introduction,
covering his dark roots with a protective hand. I assured him

that I wasn't. "I wish to Christ I'd had the presence of mind to bleach this absolute mess before getting myself locked up in here."

"Maybe they have Sharpies," I offered. "If you can't bleach the roots, darken the rest."

"Well, hello Mrs. Thinking Outside the Box! I like that in a woman."

Friendships in a Place are weird, too deep and too shallow all at once. You already know one incredibly heavy detail about the person picking at their pudding next to you, and they know you know, on top of which they know the same thing about you—but neither of you can acknowledge it. In a Place, as in prison, it's pretty gauche to ask your comrades what they're "in" for. So you keep conversation on a vapid plane and hope the good stuff comes out on its own. The vibe is like speed dating in Jonestown, or doing a fun icebreaker exercise with the hostages during a bank robbery.

Hospital life. There was TV, always tuned to what appeared to be the Maury Povich Channel. A blackboard outside the TV room tantalized us all with its claim that a showing of *Varsity Blues* would happen here soon, though no date was specified, and one of the Junkies who was on the ward for the second time that year said the same blackboard had promised the same showing of *Varsity Blues* six months ago. We latched on to this. We grew desperate for *Varsity Blues*. Those of us who'd seen it wrote checks on its behalf that it could never hope to cash: It was legendary, it was crucial, it was a tentpole of '90s cinema. We were being robbed! How could our treatment hope to progress under such deprived conditions?

We could read, but I didn't have any of my books and had chosen to be snobby about the Place's extensive collection of chicken soups for women's and teenagers' and Canadians' souls.

We could do crafts—that is, if we *could* do crafts, because despite the grandly named Arts & Crafts Corner of the day room, most crafts employed at least one tool (scissors, thread, yarn) that was forbidden on the ward. In that Corner, all most of us did was color.

Coloring was, by far and for lack of any better alternatives, the most popular activity in the Place. As a kid, I remember liking to color: selecting colors for Princess Ariel's hair (never red, always green or blue, because I was a badass) and the careful inside-the-linesing that followed (not too badass, now, can't get carried away). What a fool I was! It turns out coloring is the most boring thing in the world. Diligently shading in pictures of Disney princesses with crayons at the age of twenty-one makes you feel like a spooky weirdo, on top of which I was bad at it, too sad and fuzzy-brained to produce a halfway decent picture. You can't imagine the shame of being a shitty colorer in a place where there's nothing to do but color. I peeked at my fellow patients' projects with envy. The Junkies were better at coloring than the Crazies, broadly speaking, though the Crazies were more enthusiastic.

I wasn't the only one who was disillusioned with the one activity that was reliably on offer at the Place. The ward was full of people coloring with total focus for forty-five seconds at a time before sneaking their pages back into the stack and staring off into space instead. The most common expression on the face of someone returning to their seat from the stack of coloring books was one of supreme dissatisfaction. Residents who'd done time in other Places spoke longingly of this or that mental health Elysium where fresh coloring books arrived by the truckload every morning, still warm from the printer. Other institutions had drama clubs and aromatherapy chambers. Their cafeterias were catered by Wolfgang Puck. They showed *Varsity Blues* three times a week—no, three times a day!

You might think it's not possible to cry because you hate coloring so much, but one thing I learned at the Place was that it's possible to cry for any reason, and no reason, and all day long, and for a week straight. I learned about an obscure feeling that isn't sorrow or misery. There is an emotion called crying and it was made for Places like this. I knew, based on the conditions of my life and where they had led me, that I was unhappy, but I'd exhausted my ability to feel it. I cried without knowing why, and I cried when I remembered why, and then I cried about what a crybaby I was. Sadness needs characters and a plot. Crying, I learned, needs only a vacuum to fill.

At various points, I have been diagnosed with depression and bipolar disorder and, depending on which diagnosis was in the lead at the time, prescribed Prozac, Lexapro, Zoloft, Seroquel, Wellbutrin, Cymbalta, Trintellix, and lithium. That's not a complete list but those are the pills whose effects I remember most clearly: Cymbalta, which I stopped taking after puking it up every day for two weeks; Wellbutrin, which made me twitch and sweat; Seroquel, which made me sleep twelve hours a day and double-fist cupcakes when I was awake. I longed to treat the sickness, whatever it was, but it seemed the only way to find a medicine that worked was to torment me first with pill after pill that didn't.

I switched doctors often. When it came to prescribing medicine for my body, any jerkoff with a medical degree would do. But I was protective of my brain, and judged most doctors who tried to help me treat its illnesses as snobbish and arrogant. Either that, or they believed I was trying to pull one over on them.

"You say you've seen several doctors already this year," one of them said, closing my chart and looking at me coolly. "Perhaps you could describe to me what, exactly, you're looking to accomplish."

"I don't know," I said thickly through my woozy Seroquel haze. "It keeps not working out."

"Why isn't it working out?"

"I'm always tired. I didn't used to be so tired."

"You're looking for something that will make you feel awake? Is that what you're telling me?"

"No—I don't know," I said, confused. The pill made it hard to think clearly, and my memory of what we'd been talking about had already turned hazy. "*Is* that what I'm telling you?"

I couldn't help but notice how many of my doctors seemed only to trust other doctors. My word counted for nothing in a psychiatrist's office. This was a tricky business, because sometimes, I *was* lying—most straightforwardly when I engaged in explicit drug-seeking behavior. My husband encouraged me in this endeavor, and I figured that if doctors were going to talk to me like I was a lying criminal anyway, I might as well be one. He, for his part, adored his psychiatrist, who saw him for ten minutes a month and sent him away with large quantities of Adderall and Klonopin. A couple months before my suicide attempt, he recommended I figure out a similar setup with the next doctor I tried, so that we could double our stock of Adderall as a household. This was presented to me as a rare investment opportunity, one that might even ("who knows?") benefit my mental health, which we both knew could use some benefiting.

I came to excel at every type of psychiatric lie. I downplayed the severity of my suicidal ideation so that I wouldn't be reported as a danger to myself. I admitted only to drinking "three to four drinks per week," doing other drugs "rarely" or "never." I sanded the splinters off my thoughts when I described them, aiming always for that sweet spot: sick enough to warrant medication, not so sick as to be sent, against my will, to the hospital.

The secondary effect of all this truth-stretching was that even I struggled to see just how sick I was. Because I hadn't been honest with the medical professionals, it was dangerous to be honest with myself. What if I let the wrong thing slip in a doctor's appointment, described my pain using some triggering word or other, and got myself involuntarily committed? I was terrified of the mental hospital. For one thing, I thought it was for people who were *crazy*-crazy, not people like me who were a little sick and mostly just in want of Adderall to play with. More importantly, if I went to the hospital, my husband would have at least one delicious week alone. So would everyone else in my life, and everyone not in my life, for that matter. The world would move while I, imprisoned in a Place, would not. I didn't want to let anyone do anything without me.

Towards the end of my second day in the Place, my husband brought me a duffel bag full of clothes, books, and toiletries. Visiting hours were nearly over, and the contacts I'd worn in the ambulance were disintegrating in my eyes. I tried not to be angry for how long he'd taken to do this. It gratified me, at least, that he was a fucking wreck, that he didn't look like he'd slept once in the forty-eight hours since I'd come here. It also helped that his handsomeness drew approving stares from the other patients, even the snootiest of the Junkies.

That's right, I thought. *On the outside, I am a sexy person.*

"It's nice here," he said, hugging me. Lord, but I had missed his smell—cigarettes on top of fresh dry-cleaning.

"It's not that nice," I said.

Across the room, Kieran sat with his parents and boyfriend. He mouthed *Is that him?* When I nodded, he mimed fanning himself.

"I really miss you," my husband said, his voice breaking.

"I miss you, too." I was surprised. I hadn't seen or heard from him in two days, despite my repeated phone calls. I'd assumed that he was spending his time alone blissed-out on his lack of wife, fucking his mistress in my bed with the curtains open. At no point had it occurred to me that my suicide attempt, poorly executed as it was, had genuinely shaken him. But here he was, his face more open than I'd ever seen it, teary and haggard and guileless.

"I brought you *Infinite Jest*," he said. "I don't know. Is that dumb? I figure, you have all this time to read . . ."

"No, it's not dumb," I said. "I'll be the best-read bitch in this place."

That got a death rattle of a laugh. "Being in that apartment without you . . ." He tried to set his quivering mouth. "Like, I can't even make myself get in our bed."

"Whose bed are you getting into, then?"

As soon as the words were out of my mouth, I regretted them. To this day, I regret them. He'd been trying to call a time-out to our ongoing psychosexual mind game, and this was the mean and clumsy way I told him the game was back on. His lips stilled, he sat up straight. When the supervising nurse called an end to visiting hours, he gave me a stiff hug goodbye and left.

After dinner, I called him to apologize. His voice was syr-upy, his words were full of tongue, his tone was flat. He told me before I could say anything that the car was totaled and he wouldn't be able to visit me anymore. That was how he phrased it, "was totaled." Like the car had gone out joyriding by itself.

"Everybody's fine," he said ludicrously. "Nobody's hurt."

"I . . . what . . ." I tried to collect myself. It was my name on the lease for that car. "What *happened*?"

He hung up on me, which was just as well.

I headed to the empty dayroom to cry. I couldn't stop replay-ing my husband's visit in my head, torturing myself by taking the other fork in the road this time, responding with warmth instead of bitterness when he told me how hard it was for him to be in that apartment alone. How much would it have cost me, playing along just once? The Place is good for this sort of spiraling—you've got nothing to do, so you lock yourself in the movie theater of your brain, where the only film that's ever showing is about how you're the most hateful piece of shit in the world. I queued up that old classic and huddled into a corner to watch it.

But then . . . could it be? . . . yes! I would *not* be watching the I Hate Myself Follies tonight! Because there it was, wedged between the sofa and the wall; I may have actually rubbed my eyes in disbelief. Unable to trust myself, I called for Kieran, who gratefully abandoned a coloring book to confer with me.

"No fucking way," he said, holding up the *Varsity Blues* VHS box in reverence. "Get the others. Get everyone you can. We still have two hours before lights out."

This was no simple bossiness on his part. This was, we understood, an order from on high, for which Kieran was merely the human channel. We had found it. We had actually found it!

I galloped through the Place's halls, Paul Revere in grippy socks. *Varsity Blues* showing before bed! For real this time! This was to be our Attica. We Crazies had taken matters into our own hands. We would rely no longer on the spurious claims made by lying staffers on outdated blackboards. When I told the Junkie who had first explained that the movie night was bogus, her eyes shone. "I can't believe it," she whispered.

"They're coming," I told Kieran, breathless upon my return. "They're stoked."

He removed the video from the box, and that's when we saw it: the film unspooling wildly from the cassette, scratched and torn, unwatchable.

"Maybe you don't need to get back to him," my dad said gently when my parents visited. "Maybe you spend the rest of your time here making a plan to get away from him."

He'd suggested something similar the day of my attempt, but I hadn't been in any state to hear it. Seventy-two hours out from the dire mood of that day, I was in much better shape.

"Don't you think you're in better shape because *he* isn't with you?" my mother asked, unable, as she had been since the day she first met my husband, to keep the venom out of her voice when she referred to him.

"Yes," I admitted. "Of course. But what am I supposed to do? I have to finish school. The lease on our apartment is in his name."

"You could take the year off from school, move back home. Go back once you're feeling better."

This was my worst-ever mental health crisis, but not the only one I'd ever had, and so I knew how easy it was for my caring, protective parents to suggest this sort of solution to me. My life itself, stripped of everything I chose to adorn it with, was the most important thing to them—they would be happy to shove aside my schooling, marriage, or jobs if it meant I would live another day. But what would my life mean *to me* without any of the institutions that populated it? They wanted me to keep breathing; I did not want to only be kept breathing. If I left school in the midst of a mental health crisis, something I'd already been forced to do once, I knew I would never go back.

The problem was that they had taken me at my word that his cheating was the reason I was in here. I'd taken me at my word about that, too, at first. It was true in the sense that I wouldn't have attempted suicide if such an obvious reason hadn't announced itself at a convenient time. And it helped that I really was in one suicide attempt's worth of agony about our miserable marriage. But the pain hadn't exactly been driving the car that day; it had been more like the green light, giving me permission to go. I took my foot off that brake myself, and anything could have made me do it. Hell, I was cheating on him, too—mistreatment was just the language our marriage spoke through us.

I'd been promoting the perfectly reasonable logic that I tried to kill myself because he abused me. That was the easiest story to tell: A + B = C. Really, though, I loved him primarily because our relationship gave me so many reasons to want to kill myself. If I took him out of the equation, I wanted it for no reason at all.

There were three levels of institutional oversight at the Place, which were explained to us patients using acronyms that I've forgotten. In essence, those levels were: Suicide Watch (Scary), Suicide Watch (Normal), and Starbucks Group.

I was on Suicide Watch (Scary) for my first two nights, meaning staff members checked on me every thirty minutes no matter what. Even if I was sleeping, I had to open my eyes and wave hello, non-suicidally. After two days of sane behavior, I graduated to Suicide Watch (Normal), the same level as the majority of other patients, meaning we were under less suspicion of wanting to die, but not a lot less.

Starbucks Group, or S.G., was what Kieran and I were really after. Every afternoon, a bored nurse escorted a tiny group of patients who had been deemed low-risk to a Starbucks-branded kiosk in the hospital cafeteria, after which the gaggle went outside to mill about with their Frappuccinos. The outdoor courtyard was visible from the floor the Place was on, so that we could stare at our peers as they shuffled uncertainly between benches. They knew their outdoors time was a prize, but didn't seem to know exactly what to do with it. This was maddening for those of us locked up inside. Kieran and I watched our team floundering out there, both of us appalled at their poor maneuvering and yelling "Come the fuck on!" until an orderly told us to cut it out.

Nobody knew exactly how to get designated low-risk enough to join Starbucks Group. Obviously, telling your doctor you no longer wanted to die was a must, but I began offering florid avowals of happiness to mine as soon as I learned about S.G., and this alone wasn't enough. Kieran was working in a more Freudian vein—he believed he needed to say some specific thing about his childhood or his relationship with his mother, which would trigger his doctor to recommend him to the S.G. nurse. We worked towards our goal, comparing notes and strategies, staring covetously down at our comrades in the courtyard every day and bullshitting about what we'd do When We Got S.G.

"Right there," I said, pointing to the one bench that wasn't under a tree and was therefore free of sparrow turds. "That's the VIP section. That's where I'll sit when I get S.G."

"Girl, be serious. Look how white you've gotten in here. You'll burn to a crisp."

"You can sit next to me in the VIP section. I'll sit in your shadow."

"Mm-mm. When I get S.G.," he said grandly, his hand sweeping over the whole stunted vista of the courtyard, "you won't see me sitting for a *minute*. Not for one second!"

"Okay, so you'll do jumping jacks or whatever behind my bench, and I'll sit there, and bask in the breeze from your aerobics movements."

"Can't run around during S.G.," said one Junkie who had clearance to join Starbucks Group but had gone only once. "Guy got yelled at yesterday for walking too fast, even. Shit is *boring*."

We glared at the Junkie. He put up his hands and backed away.

"When I get S.G., I won't get any candy-ass Frappuccino, I'll tell you that much," I said, resuming the game. "I'm sick of the coffee in this place. I want the darkest roast they have, served black."

"All I want is a hot chocolate," Kieran said, his voice suddenly full of desperation, which threw me. The game was to yearn wildly in your heart for S.G. while hiding how badly you wanted it beneath layers of scorn and irony. "All I want is *one hot chocolate*. How fucking hard would it be, letting me out of here for that?"

I didn't know what to say. I looked around for staff and then touched his shoulder, a level of physical contact that we weren't allowed. He put an arm around me and sighed.

I felt the same way, even though I met with my assigned doctor every day and had daily group therapy besides. I didn't have the willpower to do the Place properly, refusing to be discharged until I truly felt better. I'd come here in that spirit, but it didn't take long for me to feel bored and deprived. During group ther-

apy, I avoided sharing as much as possible. If the therapist point-
edly called on me, which he wasn't supposed to do but regularly
did, I made something up. Something in the vein of *Yes, I'm still
sick and I'm still sad, but I'm getting better, I promise.*

On the day of my discharge, our group therapy leader asked me,
as he asked everyone, what my first non-Place meal would be. I'd
been excited about this interview for days. Everyone's answers
were so lyrical, so full of longing and desire. The power of
poetry—you could practically feel *their* Red Lobster cheddar bis-
cuits melting on *your* tongue. You gave a mouthwatering answer
to this question as a service to the people you were leaving
behind, who could hope for nothing grander than a chocolate
pudding cup for dessert rather than a hated butterscotch one.

At the moment of truth, though, I felt defeated by my own
suicide attempt and its pitiful aftermath. Whatever was supposed to happen in the Place to help a person, it hadn't happened to me, and now it never would. "A bowl of cream of crab
soup," I said flatly, ignoring the other patients' eager smiles,
until I caught Kieran's eye and felt the stinginess of my answer.
"Oh . . . and a hot chocolate. With extra, *extra* whipped cream.
Since I never got to join Starbucks Group."

I don't know if you've ever had the pleasure of announcing
to a roomful of people that you're about to consume approxi-
mately three full cups of heavy whipping cream on a hot summer's day, but I recommend it.

My husband picked me up an hour later in a borrowed car
from which the Eric Clapton song "Cocaine" was booming. I
wondered as I got into the car whether we'd talk about, you

know . . . it. Everything that had happened all week; everything he did, and I did, and the mess we two had made of our lives, a mess I'd badly wanted to make and now couldn't handle. This seemed like the moment for a candor we'd never shared, the sort that would have made it difficult to fuck and fight with our signature abandon. This was the moment to make our relationship—what was left of it—real.

We didn't talk about it. I detest Eric Clapton.

The problem was that a Place can only help a person who wants help. Help is tough and not very sexy. It means follow-ing rules. What I wanted then was shapeless and menacing, a rumble throbbing in my ears from a pool I'd found myself submerged in, one whose bottom I couldn't see. I don't know exactly what it was, though it still faintly calls my name some-times in those moments when I miss my train or cause an awk-ward silence. But I'm glad I haven't answered it since.

A month after my discharge, my husband and I were leaving a California Pizza Kitchen, holding the door for a couple walking in, when . . .

"Rax?"

It was Kieran and his boyfriend. If he hadn't had so many distinctive tattoos, I never would have recognized him. He was as tan as I now realized he was meant to be, not sallow like he'd been under the Place's unforgiving lights. He'd bleached the dark roots from his hair and slicked it into a firm high pom-padour, the better to show off the fade he hadn't been able to maintain on the ward. I was tan, too, and groomed, and be-sundressed, and no longer trapped in grippy socks.

His boyfriend recognized me and smiled warmly; my husband didn't, and didn't.

We rocked back and forth in our hug, slapping each other's backs. Happy to see each other, but more than that: happy to see the beauty to which each of us had been restored upon leaving the hospital. He made a joke about drinking a hot chocolate in this ninety-degree scorcher, I recommended one of CPK's many chicken dishes with pasta. He sipped cheekily from the raspberry iced tea I'd taken to go. We laughed, I imagine too heartily. Nothing was that funny, but God how we loved the sight of each other's faces bathed in real sunshine!

After such a raucously affectionate greeting, we didn't have much to say to each other, Kieran and I. Not in a bad way—we were serene about it, we parted ways quickly. If we ran into each other again, we wouldn't hug like that. This friendship was complete. It belonged to a Place we both hoped we'd put behind us forever; by seeing each other again in the outside world, seeing what each other's lives were properly like, we'd sewn it shut.

"Who was that?" asked my husband as we walked towards our car. The rest of our day together stretched ominously before us.

"We were in the hospital together," I said, and he whipped his head around to look at Kieran again—no, to gawk. It was an expression I would come to know well because I saw it every time I admitted to another person that I'd spent time in a mental institution. He wanted to know what crazy looked like.

Domesticating the Wolf of Wall Street

Infamous Wall Street trader Jordan Belfort was born in 1962 and raised in Bayside, Queens, in the days before his pump-and-dump schemes made him a multimillionaire. His parents were accountants, their debilitatingly middle-class jobs leading Belfort to describe himself, in his memoir *The Wolf of Wall Street*, as a "poor kid." He isn't tall and classically beautiful like Leonardo DiCaprio, who plays him in the Martin Scorsese film based on his book, but he isn't bad-looking, either. Miller model Nadine Caridi, his second wife, must have figured when she married him that she could do a helluva lot worse, rich-husband-wise. Oh, probably they loved each other—inasmuch as love is even possible when that many millions of dollars' worth of drugs and white-collar crime are the focus of a man's life.

Actually, the real Belfort has a cameo in the film as an emcee, and the cameo is illuminating: he sizzles with shrill, bug-eyed, please-like-me energy. He's affably short and suspiciously tan. He's Jewish, but doesn't read as the "savage Jew" that he repeatedly calls himself in his books. I consider his heavy Queens accent and tendency to slouch, his inability to complete a sentence without dissolving into a jumble of unintelligible syllables, and the Jewish archetype that comes to mind instead is the nebbish. He is, in short, a classic addict: the insecure guy who bought and snorted and banged his way into an approximation of cool. So did I, so did we all.

The way he buzzes about, a fly trapped under a glass, is unsettlingly relatable even if the grand mythology of his life is not. Surely I'm not the only addict who recognizes my jitters in his. An addict's life is one of peering around corners, anxiously needing—*needing!*—to know what's next. And what's next must always be bigger than what's now, more colorful and therefore more worthwhile to us. Reality is just a gray-brown animal dumbly eating acorns in the park. Drug addicts fear the neutral tones, the chores and family obligations, that comprise that deadliest of all possible things: a decent life.

The dream of every addict is to fend off, for as long as possible, the wretched caesura of boredom between fixes. Sobriety is the birthplace of boredom, as far as we're concerned, and so the mission at hand is to reduce one's drug-free downtime to the absolute minimum. And to give credit where it's due, Belfort seems to have come closer to this ideal than just about anyone else. Unlike most of us, who have no choice but to turn our attention away from drug use once in a while, he had the money and the resources to stay high twenty-four hours a day—or, if not actively high, then at least embroiled in the druggy sidequests that constitute much of an addict's life. He never ran out of people to get fucked-up with, obscure intoxicants to hunt down, parties to put a gilded edge on the encroaching unavoidable misery. I was a JV drunk, a Little League cokehead, neither able nor willing to take the large-scale risks that separate the rookies from the pros. I had no choice but to submit to the drug fiend's native boredom once in a while; Jordan Belfort's life was anti-bland for years on end, until the boredom of sobriety claimed him.

While abusing Visine and aspirin, two drugs that offer no psychotropic payoff, Belfort realizes for the first time that the payoff isn't even the point; the abuse is. Misusing a drug, any drug, is its own reward. This is a throwaway moment in the book—he lingers on this glimmer of clarity for a fraction of the time he spends reconstructing an inspiring speech he gave his employees later that day. But I read that moment over and over, seeing the tip of something crucial poking out of the dirt, something I needed to excavate. I related deeply to the impulse to abuse aspirin for no reason, and now I had to know why.

The boredom was why. Those rather desperate Visine-and-aspirin moments are, for an addict, merely more delicious sidequests to expand our sense that we're living fuller and brighter lives than everybody else. The more pointless scumbag shit we can find to fill the time, the better. It's rarely better than boredom, but always livelier.

My ex-husband once taught me that, after snorting any drug, the best thing to do was sniff deeply from a Benzedrex anticongestion inhaler. That's what Kerouac did, he explained. The inhalers no longer contained the stimulant Benzedrine that had made them attractive to Kerouac, but they did contain menthol that stung in the nostrils and (my ex said) augmented one's high.

So for years, that's what I did: snort and whiff, snort and whiff, my nostrils tingling with menthol chill.

Materially, the Benzedrex contributed nothing. In fact, my overuse of it left me with chronically freezer-burned nostrils, no good for maintaining a coke binge. No matter: the procedure itself was what I liked. It made me feel crafty, like here was this druggy Easter egg that even other users didn't know about. That crafty feeling cut through the boredom of life like nothing else, making me think I could cure that dreadful feeling entirely if I seized, always, every form of control that was available, no matter how petty.

Problematically, the boredom of life often originates in illness or pain, both of which limit your possibilities and convince you that you're missing out. What could be more boring than being laid out with a back injury—and what could belong more completely to the grind of a mature adult life than managing that pain responsibly? Easier and more exciting to take a pill for that back pain, one you decided on yourself. After all, there's so little excitement in this injured half-life that you're trapped in right now. What's the harm? Except the pain persists, and your wife suggests visiting a doctor, which you know you should. But your mind, so shrewd a chemist when it gets to call the shots about pills and doses, shuts down when it imagines the doctor's stinginess with same. Instead, you try *two* pills, then three, and when things don't improve you titrate another couple drugs into the mix, all of which must be combined and dosed in a precise, intelligent way, and your wife leaves you. What? When did she get that into her head? Has it really been a year since you first noticed this pain?

Belfort understands this thought process better than anyone. His addiction to quaaludes, a drug that is no longer available thanks to its abuse-friendliness but that was once a widely pre-scribed sedative, began with a very real lower-back injury. The injury didn't make it into the movie except as a rakish aside, when DiCaprio's Belfort puts "back pain" in scare quotes as the reason for his many dishonorably obtained prescriptions. But in the book the injury is scare-quoteless and severe. The pain generates the boredom of missing out on a full life, and the high provided by the painkillers comes to represent that fullness. And on and on the cycle goes—beginning and ending, always, with boredom.

Many of the film's critics claim that Scorsese and DiCaprio have made Belfort's life look too good. Writing for *Vulture,* David Edelstein describes the movie as "three hours of horrible people doing horrible things and admitting to being horrible," then goes on to suggest that Scorsese is trying to convince audiences to envy those horrible people their awfulness rather than embrace their own humdrum lives as "wage slaves." (Edelstein's words, not Scorsese's.) *The New Yorker's* David Denby notes the film's intent to expose "disgusting, immoral, corrupt, obscene behav-ior" and suggests that in offering a non-didactic view of that behavior, it is itself guilty of disgusting obscenity. By refusing to show Belfort's world as the colorless tragic spiral we expect from stories of addiction (and crime, for that matter), Scorsese has glamorized it. By filling that world with the same skinny blondes and sleazy idiots who really did populate Belfort's life, Scorsese is somehow forcing us to desire that life ourselves.

I believe two things to be true about people who see *The Wolf of Wall Street* through this lens: One, they themselves desire lives full of skinny blondes, sleazy idiots, and drug-addled abdication of all boredom. And, two, these are things they don't *want* to want. Safer, they may think, to avoid putting such ideas in people's heads at all, lest they be seduced into bailing on their responsibilities, pursuing Belfort's boredom-free life.

Such critiques miss the point. This film is *about* boredom: how repellant it is, the pitiable ways we try to conquer it. In the early scene where Jordan gets a blow job in his Ferrari, a cocaine mustache encrusting his lip and a fifth of bourbon sloshing in his stomach, he's simply trying to speed away from every tedious thing that's chasing him. It's natural to envy him for fleeing in style, but the boredom will eventually outrun him.

Consider the scene two-thirds of the way through the movie when Jordan's sidekick Donnie divvies up a batch of rare, exorbitantly expensive quaaludes for them to share. They take their pills, salivating over the experience they're about to have, all the more precious because most people couldn't get their hands on this drug even if they knew it existed. But the pills don't kick in, and they don't kick in, and what are these two titans of capital doing that whole time? Slumping on the sofa watching *Family Matters* in designer sweatpants and asking each other that fatal question: "Do you feel anything yet?" Sub in *30 Rock* for *Family Matters,* and it's the way I spent most of the 2010s.

Addiction is, in this limited sense, an equalizer. As long as you're in thrall to your substance(s) of choice, more money won't buy you that much better of a life. Better set-dressing and fewer life-or-death traumas to manage, yes—part of the reason people think *The Wolf of Wall Street* glamorizes Belfort's addiction is that it depicts the lavish circumstances under which it took place. But does Scorsese really make the case that Belfort got any contentment out of his expensive toys? All they ever did was give him ideas for even more expensive toys to buy once the next million-dollar check cleared, toys that would snuff out his boredom for good. The sofa he sank into was softer than mine, the TV he watched bigger, the drugs he ingested purer. But even the richest addicts on earth can't escape the imperative to sit around waiting for the fun to start.

Like Belfort, I had my favorite drugs, but I would have drunk or snorted anything. This approach allowed me the questionable pleasure of quitting several times without *quitting*-quitting, always certain that this time, finally, I'd excised the right tumor. The cancer was heroin or coke, not my refusal to live the same halfway decent life that everybody else lives.

A month before I quit coke, the last "hard" drug in my rotation, I watched a remarkable sunset with Sean, the sort that everyone on the sidewalk stops to admire. Then I wrote the following in my journal about it:

> *the sunset was a sunset. what more is there to say about a fucking sunset*

How unhappy I must have been, that I was so closed off to the idea of . . . what? Loving a sunset too much? But what kind of cornball really *loves* a sunset, I thought snottily, as if anybody in the world is too good for the sky. I was adrift on the doldrums, and snapping at all my loved ones, and brimming over with self-obsessed despair. In that moment, floating on a terrible sea with no current, I would never have risked saying something I meant. The things I meant were *boring*. Life was boring. I needed to be better than life.

Though we addicts look like we're up for anything, we are in fact a prim and prudish bunch, grossed out by any person who isn't afraid to be their dull real self. The richest addicts among us can present their lives as tedium-free, but what they really are is risk-free, emotionally speaking. We hang out with other addicts because it's logistically easier—when you're operating with such tortured brain cells, it often takes three people to remember the dealer's address. But also, it's a relief, being able to pool our shared cowardice about feelings, using drugs to induce sentimental and self-destructive versions of the emotions whose calls we otherwise refuse to hear. In cloistering ourselves within cocoons of anti-boredom, we're trying to lock out our feelings of deprivation. If we can't hear them, the reasoning goes, maybe they'll go away.

When I tell people I've gotten sober, some of them express a form of admiration that drives me up a fucking wall. "Good for you," they say, awed, worshipful. "I could *never* do that." In the film, Donnie puts it much the same way, minus the worshipfulness: "I can't imagine ever not enjoying getting fucked-up." The idea, I suppose, is that sober people are monks or nuns, creatures of pure asceticism. We have forsworn an experience of great value in the material world, and it's made us into something not quite human. In getting sober, we are announcing for all to hear our willingness, finally, to just be bored.

One problem with art that describes addiction—a problem that informs all those critics' distaste for *The Wolf of Wall Street*—is that it's nigh on impossible to make sober life sound as interesting as the life it replaces. Casual sex with intriguing beauties, uninhibited euphoria, all-night parties, riotous laughter: even if you don't use drugs yourself, even if you go to bed at nine o'clock every night, you probably agree that these things are all unambiguously appealing. Maybe a voice is whispering to you *Fuck it, she's right, let's find some trouble to get into tonight*. It's certainly whispering to me as I write this. In contrast, what would even be the central image of a sober-night-out montage? Eating too much ice cream and setting an alarm for a sensible hour?

Just about everything that makes sober life better than its alternative happens gradually, on the inside of a person. I mean, most people do look much better after being sober for a while—but if you can't take your newly glowing skin to a bar and drunkenly seduce a stranger with it, what's the point? And in the meantime, while your life is supposedly improving, every minute of it is dilating. It's not that you never feel good; it's that the good feelings now burble up so slowly to the surface of your bog, leaving you mired in monotony the rest of the time. In the film, Donnie asks the newly sober Jordan how his drug-free life is going. Jordan replies, "It fucking sucks. It's so boring I want to kill myself."

I had that phase, too—when the boredom of sobriety made me want to die because I hadn't yet noticed how much better I was living. In that first year, I obsessed, often, over a certain house in my neighborhood. It was an ugly place with aluminum siding and a sagging porch, totally without note until its violet porch light came on at 5 P.M. That's when I arranged to walk my dog most days, so that we could watch the hordes of skinny people in skinnier jeans as they shambled up the house's creaking porch steps in twos and threes, looking at no one, worrying at their scabby limbs.

I did not want to go in there, exactly. But it thrilled me to imagine that I could, in a way that abstinence from drugs otherwise failed to thrill me. My life was no longer filled with scumbag side-quests. It got stark, and slow. This was the back door I left open in the rickety shack of my sobriety: If it got too boring, I could always heed the call of the violet lamp. Stay an hour, stay an evening, leave with a few scabs of my own to pick. No one would ever have to know I'd done it.

"I don't get why you would do that," Sean said when I admitted my secret desire for the house. At this point, I had been sober almost a year. "After all the progress you've made."

"What progress? I wake up, I work, I putter around the house with you and the dog. When I'm really feeling wild, we go out and feed the ducks. What progress!"

"It's officially getting weird," he said, "that I can tell how much happier you are this way, and you can't."

Goofily enough, this was the first time I'd thought about my quitting in terms of my happiness, rather than my health or responsibilities. I mostly saw sobriety as just some tedious homework I had to do. But that remark made me realize that I couldn't even remember the last time I'd *wept*. I used to weep all the time—the high melodrama of an addict's life means spending a lot of time sobbing. But when had I last wanted to die for reasons I didn't even understand? Or picked a fight with Sean?

When was the last time I'd gotten so angry that my bellowing had frightened the dog, and then collapsed into tears because my poor dog was afraid of me? My life was no longer a jagged line connecting one crisis to the next. This was the first time I'd thought to feel grateful for the boredom—for everything it had so calmly replaced. Maybe the word wasn't "boredom" at all, but "serenity."

"Holy shit," I said. "I *am* happier."

"Duh," he said.

Jordan Belfort doesn't seem to have learned his lesson. Though he made his fortune on Wall Street by, essentially, ripping off schmucks until he was imprisoned for it, he continues to write "insider's playbooks" for making money in the stock market and persuading other people to do what you want. He only talks about his sobriety anymore in the context of shilling on Instagram for an "ibogaine treatment center" in Cancun that costs ten thousand dollars a week. Per Belfort, ibogaine was the only thing that allowed him to get sober for good; per medical doctors, ibogaine is cardiotoxic and most clinics that offer it are wholly unregulated. On top of that, making elaborate plans to bleed people dry and get rich quick is cokehead behavior, plain and simple. The primary difference between Belfort and the guy in the bar blathering about why you should start a record label with him is only the quality of the clothes on his back while he blathers.

Is he bored? Is he happy?

Social media lies, so it's hard to say, but I can try to filter out bits of truth from his posts the same way I did from his books.

He's married to another skinny blonde who's about the same age as Nadine Caridi was when she married him, though he, obviously, is much older. He wears the same well-tailored suits, tours the world to talk about life as a big bad Wolf, and spends a lot of time reliving the glory days. In most ways, he's living as his past self as much as possible—because that's the self that makes him money, true, but also because he's still trying to outrun boredom. He can't get high anymore, but he can still bag babes and pitch stocks, dammit!

I can no longer bag the proverbial babes, nor pitch the proverbial stocks. If it was a superpower bestowed on me by drugs, it's gone now. But, crucially, I don't miss it. Almost two years into sobriety, I've finally stopped yearning for some drug-free way to re-inhabit my party girl self. When I catch myself missing her, I remember the cost of doing business with her—all the time I spent sobbing, antagonizing my loved ones, all so I could steal one more hour away from boredom.

Lately, I'm a little bit bored for most of the day. Even without drugs, there are plenty of minor naughtinesses I can wedge into those gaps of tedium. I can buy a dress I don't need, or waste time futzing around on my phone—and, often, I do. I've established, after all, that I am not a damn monk, and can't completely crush my drive to fuck up my life just a little so I don't have to sit with the starkness of it twenty-four hours a day. But I don't bolt from the stillness every time anymore. When it makes me itch, I don't always scratch. *Go ahead,* I say to my boredom instead. *You can have an hour's head start this time.*

Acknowledgments

Thank you to the men I have loved, and the women I have loved, and the people I have loved. Some of you appear explicitly in the pages of this book, others are the foundation on which I built it. I can't do jack shit without any of you and I love you all forever.

Thank you, Mutti, for always being there for me, even when I was doing all the stuff in this book, much of which I know was frustrating and horrifying to you as a mother. You remain the best and least judgmental roommate I've ever had.

Thank you, Katya, for introducing us to *The Traitors* and giving me unbelievable jewelry for every birthday and holiday. I will be buried with all of it, and with you, like a pharaoh. (Yes, I'm threatening to put you in my coffin with me. Just roll with it.)

Thank you, Amber, for our baby, by which I mean our trash podcast about trash culture, not your human baby. I mean the important one.

Thank you, Noor, Tommy, Eve, Neil, Josh, Cory, Mattie, Jaya, Chelsea, my Yiddish friends, my banjo friends, my podcasting friends, my writer friends, and all the friends I can't name who have spent the past few years showing me how much fun I can have without drugs and alcohol. I bet none of you even realized that's what you were doing. Suckers.

Thank you to my editor, Vanessa Haughton, and my agent, Kent Wolf, for bringing this book into the world like the firm yet tender midwives that you are. Without you both, I would be less a writer than a weirdo mumbling little quips to myself.

Thank you to my manager, Ali Lefkowitz, for helping me navigate Tinseltown and thanks in advance for not making fun of my referring to it as "Tinseltown."

Special gratitude is due to my literary hero, the irrepressible Lisa Crystal Carver, who was the first one to see any part of this book and highlighted huge swaths of it and told me which swaths to keep and which were unusable. You got me on the right track and no mistake. Your talent, generosity, thoughtfulness, and patience with my swaths are all unparalleled, and I truly just love your work so much. Wow, look at us, crying like a couple of girls!

Thank you to my beautiful hometown of Washington, D.C., my favorite city in the country, for turning me into . . . whatever it is that I am. You're the embarrassing uncle of cities, in that I hate so much of what you do but God help anyone from outside the family if they try to talk shit.

Finally, thank you to Sean. You just worked in the sun all day and now you're walking the dog so I can finish writing these acknowledgments uninterrupted. I love you more than anything else in the world. I have more fun cleaning the apartment with you while listening to Roger Miller records than I had in fifteen years of drunken partying. Can we get burgers again tonight?

ALSO BY

RAX KING

TACKY
Love Letters to the Worst Culture We Have to Offer

Tacky is about the power of pop culture—like any art—to imprint itself on our lives and shape our experiences, no matter one's commitment to "good" taste. These fourteen essays are a nostalgia-soaked antidote to the millennial generation's obsession with irony, putting the aesthetics we hate to love—snakeskin pants, *Sex and the City*, Cheesecake Factory's gargantuan menu—into kinder and sharper perspective. Each essay revolves around a different maligned (and yet, Rax would argue, vital) cultural artifact, providing thoughtful, even romantic, meditations on desire, love, and the power of nostalgia. An essay about the gym-tan-laundry exuberance of *Jersey Shore* morphs into an excavation of grief over the death of her father; in "You Wanna Be on Top," Rax writes about friendship and early aughts girlhood; in another, Guy Fieri helps her heal from an abusive relationship. The result is a collection that captures the personal and generational experience of finding joy in caring just a little too much with clarity, heartfelt honesty, and Rax King's trademark humor.

Essays

VINTAGE BOOKS
Available wherever books are sold.
vintagebooks.com